hook, loop & lock

create fun and easy locker hooked projects

Theresa Pulido

CINCINNATI, OHIO

www.mycraftivity.com

Connect. Create. Explore.

Other fine books from Krause Publications are available from your local bookstore, craft store or visit us at our Web site at www.fwmedia.com.

16 15 14 13 12   10 9 8 7 6

DISTRIBUTED IN CANADA BY FRASER DIRECT
100 Armstrong Avenue
Georgetown, ON, Canada L7G 5S4
Tel: (905) 877-4411

DISTRIBUTED IN THE U.K. AND EUROPE BY DAVID & CHARLES
Brunel House, Newton Abbot, Devon, TQ12 4PU, England
Tel: (+44) 1626 323200, Fax: (+44) 1626 323319
Email: postmaster@davidandcharles.co.uk

DISTRIBUTED IN AUSTRALIA BY CAPRICORN LINK
P.O. Box 704, S. Windsor NSW, 2756 Australia
Tel: (02) 4577-3555

Library of Congress Cataloging in Publication Data
Pulido, Theresa
 Hook, loop & lock : create fun and easy locker hooked projects / Theresa Pulido. -- 1st ed.
    p. cm.
 Includes index.
 ISBN 978-1-60061-129-2 (alk. paper)
 1. Locker hooking. I. Title.
 TT833.P95 2009
 746.7'4--dc22
                        2008039083

Editor: Jennifer Claydon
Designer: Julie Barnett
Production Coordinator: Matt Wagner
Photographers: Christine Polomsky and Tim Grondin

metric conversion chart

TO CONVERT	TO	MULTIPLY BY
INCHES	CENTIMETERS	2.54
CENTIMETERS	INCHES	0.4
FEET	CENTIMETERS	30.5
CENTIMETERS	FEET	0.03
YARDS	METERS	0.9
METERS	YARDS	1.1

About the Author

Theresa Pulido divides her time between her consulting business in corporate marketing and media relations, gardening, crafts and other hobbies. Theresa has always been fanatical about color—most likely an influence from her Spanish heritage. In her free time, she assists her husband with home winemaking on their 125-vine project vineyard called Giraffe Wines. They're currently working on their third vintage. Theresa lives in Sonoma, California, with her husband, Chris, and her calico kitty, Princess Keena. For more information and craft ideas visit Theresa's blog at www.colorcrazycrafts.com.

Acknowledgments

I'd like to thank everyone who has contributed to this book in various ways. I really appreciate the groundswell of support I have received—the encouragement as well as the inspiration and great ideas. Special thanks to my contributors—Kathleen Carpenter, Cathren Britt, Sherri Haab and Cindy Sadowski—for their truly creative contributions. Many thanks go out to my editor at F+W, Jenni Claydon, for her invaluable support, and to F+W's acquisitions editor, Tonia Davenport, for believing and helping to make this idea come true. My family was also incredibly supportive. A heartfelt thank you goes out to my sister Olga for helping to pull together an impromptu focus group. Even my brother Manny participated. He tried locker hooking and was quite good at it. For their valuable feedback and words of encouragement, I'd like to thank my sister Linda and my friends Olivia Wilson and Gloria Marquez. For their generous support and contributions of their fabulous products, I'd like to thank Judi Suleski at M.C.G. Textiles, Bruce Feller and Carma Ferrier at Lantern Moon, Karen Davis at Bali Fabrics, Judy Tomsky at Natural Beads and Sonnie Wendell for the swatches of luscious fabrics from Rodolph. A special thanks to Michael Katz and staff at Rupert, Gibbon & Spider, manufacturers of Jacquard Products, for all the support.

Dedication

This book is dedicated to my husband, Chris Kukshtel, for his patience, good humor and ongoing support. While producing projects for the book, I literally had fibers, fabric strips, yarn and locker hooking supplies strung out throughout our home.

contents

I came to locker hooking in an odd way: through my love of gardening. The idea of planting things that grow and can be harvested has always been appealing to me, and when I moved from fast-paced Silicon Valley to Sonoma, California, my idea to start a garden finally became a reality. In an effort to spend more time at home so I could tend the garden I took a job in Sonoma. My responsibilities there included developing and marketing a line of crafts, and it was through this effort that I was first introduced to locker hooking. I'd heard of latch hooking but had never heard of locker hooking, and the moment I saw it I was taken with it.

It's not surprising to me that most people have never heard of locker hooking. It's an obscure craft with a strange name. Locker hooking may sound like it has something to do with fishing or carpentry, but don't let the name fool you! Locker hooking is a fun craft that produces a great sense of accomplishment—it's easy to grasp and, with a little practice, you can finish a project quickly. Once I got started, I realized that locker hooking could take on a whole new life with designs that use vibrant colors, wild materials or interesting textures—both simple designs and more complex designs can be beautifully executed in locker hooking.

In her book entitled *Needlework through History: An Encyclopedia*, Catherine Amoroso Leslie writes, "Locker hooking is not as well-known as other rug techniques. Its full potential has yet to be explored by contemporary needle workers." Well, I couldn't agree more! I hope this book helps spread the word about locker hooking and generates more interest in this wonderful craft. I hope it inspires you to try something new with locker hooking. My designs and color combinations are strongly inspired by my love of gardening. The look of tilled soil, the neat rows of planted crops and the stunning array of colors all contribute to my projects. You can bring inspiration from your own life when you try these designs. Pick your favorite colors and textures for these projects. Once you've got the basics down, there's no reason you can't try your hand at creating a design of your own. Locker hooking can be used to make beautiful home decor pieces, and there's nothing like giving a handmade locker hooked gift. Try a locker hooked design to accent the dining table, or add a special touch to a room with your own rug design. This is a meditative craft, and it travels well. It can be done while listening to music, watching television or even sunning at the beach.

Just a small warning, though: Locker hooking can be addictive!

locker hooking supplies

Only a few simple materials are required to start locker hooking, and they are inexpensive and easy to find. You can purchase the necessary supplies at most craft stores or shop for them online, but don't feel like you have to stop at the basics! You can choose to use leftover scraps of fabric as traditional locker hookers have done for decades, or try a rich new look with luxurious materials like silk, satin and mohair fibers. Almost any fiber or fabric can be used for locker hooking—anything from wool to cotton and silk. You can even use strips of plastic! You can also combine fibers and locker hook them together for a unique, layered look. Once the locker hooking is done, you can take your project further with creative embellishments like beads, buttons and more. Experiment with different finds to create projects that are just your style!

Basic Locker Hooking Materials

At its most basic, locker hooking only requires three materials: a base to locker hook on, a decorative material to create your design, and a locking medium to hold your design in place. Although this may sound simple, your choices are limited only by your imagination! When choosing locker hooking materials, take your project's purpose into account. A project that takes a lot of wear and tear, such as a rug, requires sturdy materials, while a decorative item is less limited by practical concerns.

Rug canvas is the most common base used for locker hooking. Measured in squares per inch, rug canvas is widely available in two different sizes. For rugs and other large projects, I prefer the size 3.75 canvas. A size 5 canvas is also available for smaller projects. I prefer the size 5 canvas for most of my projects because it allows me to produce more detailed designs. Be sure to use the canvas size suggested in the project instructions, or the quality of your project will be compromised and it will be the wrong size when you are finished.

Burlap can also be used as a locker hooking base. While the grid structure of burlap is not as defined as rug canvas, you can create beautiful free-form designs on burlap, which provides a great organic look for locker hooking. Burlap also does not need to be completely covered in a locker hooked design to make an attractive project. Burlap is available in a variety of colors at most fabric shops.

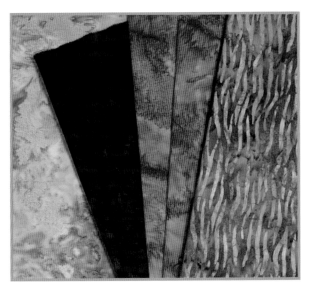

Fabric is the traditional choice for the decorative portion of a locker hooked project. If you want to make a project from cotton fabric, use quilting-quality cotton fabric that has a high thread count. It has a heavier weight and will fray less. Printed fabrics are widely available, but using them requires a little more work because each strip has to be folded to hide the wrong side of the fabric. I love using hand-dyed fabrics because they have variegated colors and both sides of the fabric are the same, unlike printed fabrics. They're a little more expensive, but I think using a handcrafted product makes them worth the price. Fabric needs to be cut into strips before it can be used in locker hooking.

Pre-cut fabric strips are a wonderful time-saver for the modern locker hooker. While using pre-cut strips is more expensive than cutting your own fabric into strips, you may decide, like I did, that the time savings is worth the extra expense. Pre-cut strips may fray more than strips you cut yourself because their edges are exposed for a longer period before you begin working with them. For some projects, you may prefer the fringed texture of a little fraying. If not, a few snips with your scissors can take care of that problem quickly!

Locking medium passes through the decorative loops in your design and holds them in place. Any strong, smooth, non-stretching material can be used to lock your loops. The traditional locking medium is cotton twine, and this is a great choice for most projects. You can also use a heavy cotton yarn, or a blend of cotton, acrylic or nylon, as long as the yarn doesn't stretch too much. Although locking medium isn't supposed to be a visible part of your design, it can sometimes show between the decorative loops, so it's a good idea to color coordinate your locking medium with the decorative loops. I usually use black yarn for colorful fabrics as it doesn't contrast sharply like white cotton twine does if it peeks through.

Specialty Locker Hooking Materials

In addition to traditional fabric strips, you can use a number of unique, interesting materials for locker hooking, from simple to luxurious. These specialty materials can be combined with traditional materials or each other to create wonderful layering effects and interesting textures. You can locker hook with anything that is flexible enough and small enough to fit through your base material. Here are a few of my favorite materials.

Yarn is a wonderful material to experiment with. It is readily available and comes in a variety of fibers, colors and textures. With so many unique novelty yarns on the market, you can go from wooly to wild. You can locker hook a heavy yarn on its own or layer a finer yarn over fabric. I like layering mohair yarn on fabric to create a fuzzy, soft texture.

Wool fabric adds a warm texture to designs. Pre-cut wool strips are available in ¼" widths (6mm) that work well for size 5 canvas. You can also choose to cut wool fabric, which is available in many colors and textures, into strips for locker hooking. Locker hooked wool fabric strips can get pilly on the edges of items that get a lot of wear.

Silk fabric adds a luxurious feel and shimmer to any locker hooked design. You can cut your own silk fabric strips, or buy pre-cut silk strips, such as the Silk Gelato yarn I use in several projects. Silk fabric strips unravel more than their cotton counterparts do, but I think the fringed edge adds great texture to a project.

Ribbon can be used as part of a locker hooked design, or as an embellishment. You can locker hook with ribbons individually or layer them over fabric strips. Ribbon is also a wonderful choice for framing a locker hooked piece. I like using sheer nylon ribbons to add a subtle touch of shimmer to any project.

Plastic strips are just one example of how materials can be transformed and recycled into a locker hooked project. Plastic bags and disposable party tablecloths can be cut into strips just like fabric and used for a unique and inventive locker hooked project. Don't stop recycling at just plastic, either. Old clothes can have new life as locker hooking materials. If you get creative and look at things around you with new eyes, you're sure to find unique additions for your projects.

Embellishments

It's easy to get carried away with embellishing. Sometimes less is more, but it all depends on the design and your style. From ultra-creative and artsy to simple and elegant, the embellishments you use give a project personality. You can add buttons, beads, charms and more to make a project "just right." Embellishing is very personal, so dig through your crafty treasure box and pick out your favorite embellishments for your projects.

Beads add sparkle or color to a project. You can use beads in a variety of materials for embellishing; glass, resin, polymer clay, wood, metal or semiprecious gems are all great choices. Resin beads are my favorite—they're shaped like candy and are available in lots of yummy colors.

Buttons can be used for their original purpose (closures) on locker hooked projects or just for decoration. If you want to add personal meaning to a project, dig into your mother's or grandmother's stash of buttons or even your own. And for a perfect match, head out to a well-stocked fabric store. The variety of buttons available today is amazing (and tempting!).

Charms are perfect for embellishing an eclectic design, and they help personalize your project. Charms are available from numerous sources in a variety of designs—some with special messages or symbols. They can be found in various materials, including metal, enamel and polymer clay. You can also make your own charms with polymer clay.

Paint isn't something you would normally see used on a locker hooked project, but it can embellish a project that goes off the beaten path. I use paint to decorate rug canvas that is left unhooked.

Glitter can add subtle shimmer, or all-out sparkle. I sometimes like to pair glitter with paint to jazz up a project, although both are great on their own. Glitter is also perfect for emphasizing other embellishments on a project.

Felt produces embellishments with a softer look and feel, and adds a touch of whimsy to a project.

Tools for Locker Hooking

The tools used for locker hooking are simple, and you can find them in most large craft stores. Try the different types of locker hooks available and choose the one that feels the most comfortable. The same goes for the other tools you use to craft. If you choose tools that are comfortable and easy for you to use, you will have a much more enjoyable time crafting.

A locker hook will be your main tool for creating the projects in this book. Constructed with a hook at one end for pulling up loops of fabric and an eye at the other for carrying locking medium, a locker hook is a unique tool. There are two types of locker hooks that are widely available: aluminum and steel. I prefer the lighter-weight aluminum hook, but one of this book's contributing artists prefers the heavier steel hook. Try both and stick with whatever feels most comfortable.

A tapestry needle comes in handy when it's time to frame a canvas piece or sew locker hooked pieces together. A tapestry needle has a blunt tip and a large eye. I recommend a size 13 tapestry needle for working with locker hooked projects.

Scissors are used for cutting canvas, strips of fabric and locking medium. Use a large, heavy-duty pair of scissors for canvas and a small, sharp pair for fabric.

A rotary cutter and cutting mat are invaluable time-savers for cutting your own fabric strips. A rotary cutter has a circular blade and is used to cut fabric like a pizza cutter is used to cut pizza. Choose a rotary cutter with a safety shield. Rotary cutter blades are extremely sharp and should be handled with care. I also recommend using a self-healing mat with a rotary cutter, although any cutting mat will do.

A ruler is very helpful in locker hooking, as it is for many crafts. You can use a ruler to measure your canvas or fabric and to mark straight lines. I like using a sturdy steel ruler.

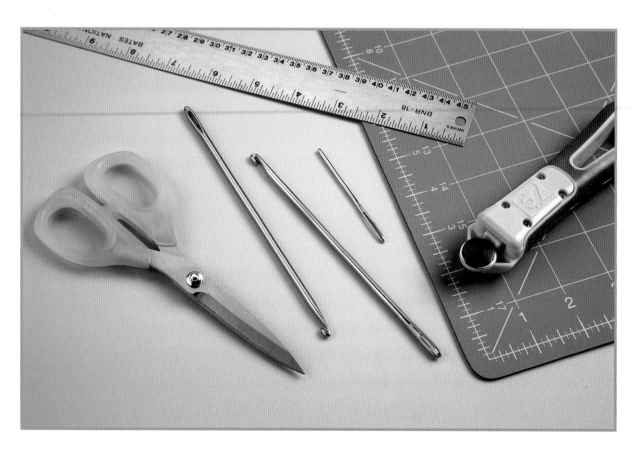

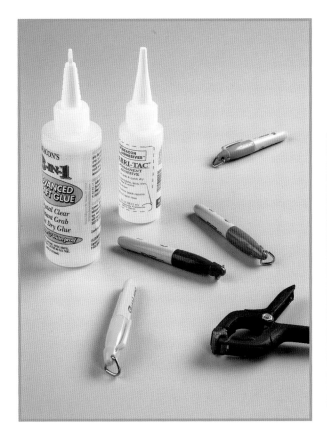

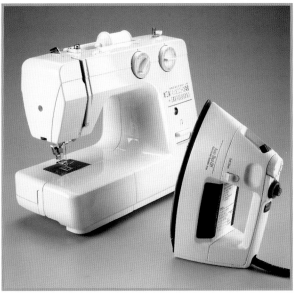

Permanent markers are perfect for marking a pattern on canvas. Marking a pattern on the canvas isn't a must, but I do recommend it for more complex patterns. You can use different colored markers for each section and color you'll be using. If you make a mistake, you can use white correction fluid to cover the incorrectly marked areas and start over once the area dries. Permanent markers and correction fluid can both be found at office supply stores.

Glue is used to help stabilize and secure your locker hooking base. Small pieces of canvas especially need the added support of glued edges. Without strong adhesive, the canvas could become unstable after hooking and could unravel. Most permanent adhesives have toxic fumes, so be sure to use them in a well-ventilated area and follow all of the manufacturer's instructions. I recommend Beacon Adhesives' Quick Grip because it dries fast, is waterproof and creates a strong bond.

A sewing machine can also be used to secure the edges of a piece of canvas. I highly recommend a machine-stitched edge when locker hooking a rug or a project that will receive a lot of wear and tear. If you don't have access to a sewing machine, you can hand stitch the edges instead.

An iron is needed for steam pressing fabric and taking creases out of burlap or linings. You will also need to have an iron handy to apply iron-on interfacing.

Clamps are useful for holding pieces together. When working in the round to finish a project, a good set of metal or plastic clamps works well to hold the canvas in place. If you're using adhesive, you can use clamps to hold pieces together until they dry.

locker hooking techniques

The basic technique for locker hooking is to pull decorative loops up through the base material, and then lock them in place with locking medium. If you're just getting started with locker hooking, I recommend that you start with a small project and focus on the traditional locker hooking technique of working in rows, otherwise known as the linear locker hooking method. Once you've learned the basics, you can use variations to create the project you desire. Learn how to pick up new colors and drop them as needed according to the pattern. Then, try different techniques, like working in a spiral or working free-form. You can work diagonally, in swirls, or create an organic design. It's also fun to combine techniques or vary the loop length for diverse textures. If you're creating your own design, experiment with different techniques to see what works best and what complements your design.

Preparing Fabric

If you use fabric yardage instead of pre-cut strips, you need to prepare the fabric for your project. Start by steam pressing the fabric to eliminate wrinkles, then cut off the selvages. Next, cut the fabric into strips. The width of strips you cut depends on the type of base material you are using, and the type of fabric you're using. The weight of the fabric makes a difference in how it will fill in a design. Cut a test strip and try it in the canvas by pulling up some loops before you continue cutting the remaining fabric. For size 3.75 rug canvas, I usually use 1" (3cm) strips of printed cotton fabric, ¾" (2cm) batik strips, or ½" (13mm) strips of thicker fabrics like wool. For size 5 rug canvas, I like to use ¾" (2cm) strips of printed cotton fabric, ½" (13mm) batik strips, or ¼" (6mm) strips of thick fabrics.

Tearing Strips

Fabric strips fray, which can create an interesting texture in your finished project, but that look isn't suitable for every project. To reduce the amount of fraying, tear your fabric into strips. Torn strips fray less than cut strips. I prefer to use this method when the fabric tears well, as it's much faster than cutting with scissors or a rotary cutter. Fabric can be torn parallel or perpendicular to the selvages.

1 Notch fabric
Spread the fabric out on a marked cutting mat or along the edge of a ruler. Cut notches along the edge of the fabric in the widths required for your project.

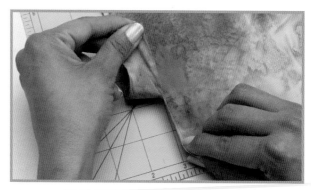

2 Tear fabric
Grasp the fabric on each side of the cut notch and pull firmly and smoothly to tear off a strip of fabric. Trim away any stray threads on the edges of the fabric.

Rotary Cutting Strips

Why use scissors when you can speed up the process with a rotary cutter? There are several good-quality rotary cutters on the market today that make cutting strips a lot easier. For quick and easy strips that are cut evenly, use a rotary cutter, a self-healing mat and a steel ruler or straightedge.

1 Cut strips
Begin by trimming the edge of the fabric so it is straight. Align the fabric on the cutting mat along one of the marked lines. Use the marked lines on the mat as a guide to align your ruler and to cut the fabric strips to the correct width. Roll the blade of the rotary cutter along the fabric next to the edge of the ruler. Be careful as you work, as rotary cutter blades are extremely sharp.

Preparing the Base

Preparing a base is as simple as measuring, cutting and marking. It is a simple process, but it is also a very important one, and good preparation will play a role in the success of your project. When preparing your base, you may also need to steam press it to eliminate any creases or wrinkles. Rug canvas is sold folded in its package and may have stubborn folds. Take the time to prepare your base correctly and you will save yourself time and frustration later.

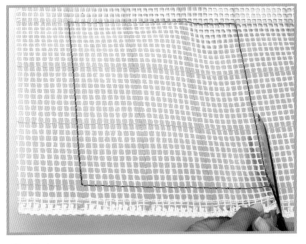

1 Measure
Measure the amount of base material needed for the project. If required, add a seam allowance to the finished measurements. For most canvas projects, add 3 squares on each side for folding over. I recommend folding over 4 squares for larger pieces like rugs and 2 for smaller pieces. Some decorative pieces won't need a seam allowance at all. The base material sizes listed for each project in this book already include the required seam allowance.

2 Cut
Use heavy-duty scissors to cut the pieces of base material. Leave neat edges without any frayed or protruding threads.

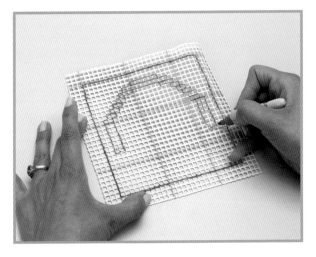

3 Mark (optional)
While not required for all designs, marking the base with your pattern can be very helpful. This makes it much easier to follow the pattern and to know when to change colors as you're working. Use permanent markers to mark your pattern on the canvas. Use markers in different colors to indicate which colors you'll be using in each section. Complex patterns are especially good candidates for marking.

Securing the Edges of the Base

It is important to ensure that the edges of a locker hooked project will stay put and will not unravel with wear and tear. There are a number of ways to secure the edges, and each has its advantages and disadvantages. Choose the correct edge treatment for your project, and it's sure to be around for years to come.

Fold edge

For most projects, folding two to four squares of canvas over and creasing it with your fingers will create enough stability and allow for a tidy framed edge. The easiest way to do this is to break a row of squares by creasing and folding in the center of the row. Follow your pattern to choose the number of squares to fold under.

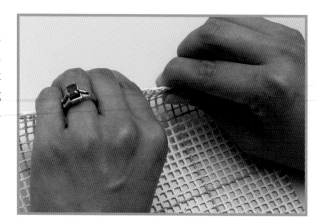

Press edge

Folding rug-hooking canvas with your fingers should be sufficient to crease the canvas. However, you may need to press burlap for it to hold the crease. Fold over the amount of burlap indicated in the project instructions. Press the fabric until it stays folded without being held.

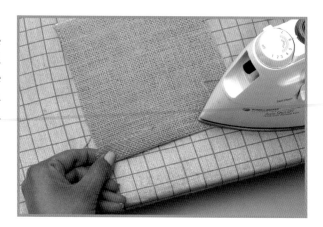

Glue edge

You can glue any folded edges down, but using glue is especially helpful on smaller pieces. If you're hooking a small piece, a strong permanent adhesive—preferably fast-drying and waterproof—adds needed stability to the edges.

Crease the canvas following the project's instructions. Apply a fast-drying, permanent, waterproof adhesive to the edge of the canvas. Hold the edge down until the glue is dry enough to hold the canvas together. Clear the canvas holes of adhesive before it dries.

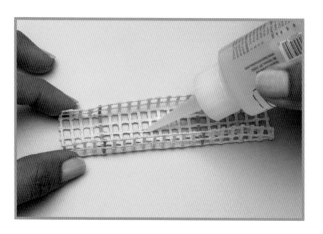

Stitch edge

Projects that will get lots of wear and tear, like rugs, require a stitched edge. The last thing you want is to have a project unravel or fall apart after it is washed. Use this step if you plan to create a design that will be machine washed or will be subjected to heavy use.

Crease the canvas along the required seam allowance. Secure the edge by stitching it with a sewing machine. Use a heavy-duty thread or tapestry thread and a zigzag stitch. If you don't have access to a sewing machine, stitch the edge by hand.

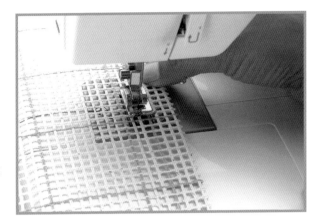

Framing the Canvas

You need to frame your canvas for projects that stand alone and are not to be assembled and sewn to other pieces. Framing allows you to fully cover the edges for a neat and tidy look. You can match the frame to the piece or use a contrasting color for the framed edge. And, as you'll see in some of the projects, you can get creative by adding fringe or other embellishments to the edge.

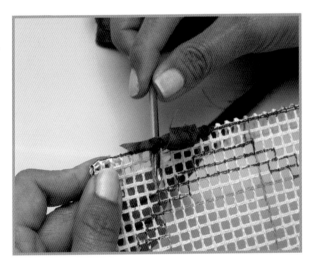

1 Start fabric strip
Fold the canvas along the project's recommended seam allowance. Cut a strip of fabric; I recommend using a strip no longer than 1½ yd. (1.5m) to avoid excess fraying. Thread the fabric strip through the eye of a locker hook or a tapestry needle. Pull the fabric strip through a square on the edge of the canvas from front to back. Leave a 2" (5cm) tail on the back of the canvas. Begin whip stitching around the edge of the canvas; whip stitch around the tail of the fabric strip as well to secure it.

2 Turning a corner
When you reach a corner, you need to stitch into the corner square twice. Stitch into the corner square when you reach it, turn the canvas, and stitch into the same square again to cover the edge of the canvas on each side of the corner. Use your fingers to spread the fabric over the corner before tightening the loop.

Basic Locker Hooking

The real fun starts here because you finally get to see your design start taking shape. These are the basic steps that are used for hooking all the projects in this book. This demonstration shows the linear method of locker hooking, but you'll learn about all the locker hooking methods on pages 24–25. The patterns in this book will instruct you as to which method to use for each project.

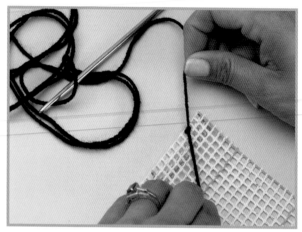

1 Attach locking medium
Prepare the edges of the canvas or burlap as needed. Cut a 2 yd. (2m) length of locking medium. Thread the locking medium through the eye of the locker hook. Tie the locking medium at the starting point of the pattern.

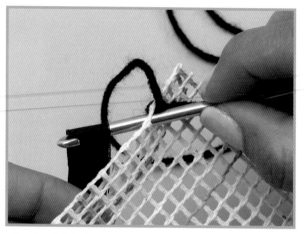

2 Hook fabric
Holding a fabric strip at the back of the canvas, push the hook from front to back through the hole in the canvas closest to the starting point of the pattern and hook the fabric.

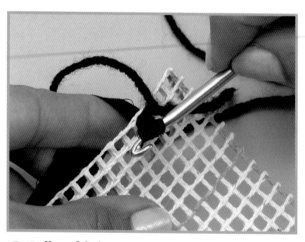

3 Pull up fabric
Pull a loop of fabric up through the canvas leaving a 2" (5cm) tail at the back of the fabric. Leave the loop of fabric on the hook.

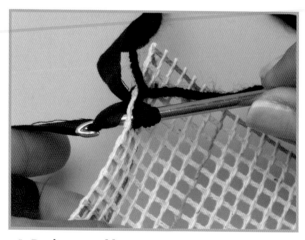

4 Begin second loop
Pass the hook through the next hole in the canvas and hook a second loop of fabric.

5 **Continue hooking**
Pull the second loop of fabric to the front. Repeat this until 4 or 5 loops of fabric are on the locker hook.

6 **Lock loops**
Pull the locker hook and locking medium through the loops on the hook. Continue picking up new fabric loops and locking the loops while following the project's design.

Loop length

Locker hooking is fun and easy, and it only takes a little practice to get the steps right. I have seen crafters who are just getting started with locker hooking get very frustrated because their loops are uneven. The best way to get comfortable is to start with a small project and to practice pulling up loops. The loops need to be at least ¼" (6mm) tall. If your loops are tall enough, your project will look great and you'll have enough room to pull up yarn or fabric tails and hide them. If your loops are too tight, you'll see the locking medium peeking out between the loops and you'll have a hard time hiding your tails.

The tension required for pulling up loops will come naturally with practice. Start by pulling up the first loop.

Make sure it is at least ¼" (6mm) tall. Pull up a second loop and give it a tug to match the height of the first loop. Since the first loop will still be on your hook, it will keep you from pulling up the second loop too much. Repeat this with the next few loops, continuing to tug with the hook to ensure consistent loop height until you have four or five loops on the hook. This will help you develop the right tension to pull up loops more easily and quickly. If you're working in the linear method, you can pull up quite a few loops at one time before pulling the locking medium through to secure them. Once you've gotten some practice, you can try patterns that call for different loop lengths—loops in different heights create a fun and funky look, while extra long loops add a decorative element.

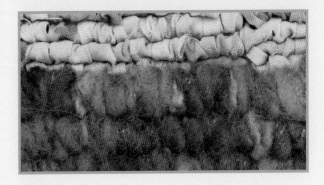

Locker Hooking Methods

There are different ways to locker hook, and the method you choose will affect the final appearance of your project. You can work in the linear method of filling in rows, working right to left, or left to right, which creates a tidy look. You can also work in a spiral, filling in the design by working in a circular fashion. This method helps the different elements of a design stand out and get noticed. The free-form method, which produces a very fun, creative project is a more organic method. Combining the methods in a design adds a wonderful sense of texture and movement to a locker hooked piece.

Linear Locker Hooking

The linear method is the most basic way to complete a locker hooked design. It's easy and faster than any other method.

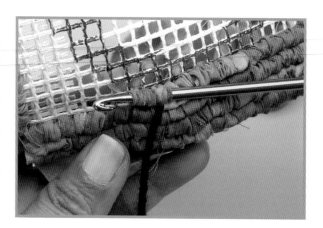

To locker hook using the linear method, start in the corner of the canvas and work straight across each row of squares, switching colors as needed to follow the pattern on the canvas (see *Switching Colors*, page 28). When you reach the end of a row, turn the piece and work the next row in the opposite direction.

Spiral Locker Hooking

The spiral method creates a swirled effect. Begin where indicated by the pattern and work in a circular fashion until you fill the entire section. You can also work in a spiral to create a frame or border around the canvas by starting at an outer corner and working inward. A spiral border is ideal for rugs because it creates a nice framed look.

1 Work across row
Start in the center of the spiral section of the pattern. Hook the number of loops required by the pattern for the first row.

2 Turn piece
Turn the piece 90° (instead of 180° for linear locker hooking) and begin working the next row. Continue hooking, turning the piece 90° at the end of each row.

Free-Form Locker Hooking

The most advanced method of locker hooking is free-form. It can be used to create wonderful textured pieces. Using free-form, you can outline different elements of the pattern on the canvas and fill them in following the natural contours of the shapes in the design. Projects really come to life with the free-form technique because of the sense of movement it creates.

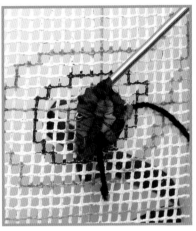

1 **Start working**
Begin free-form locker hooking at the first pattern element listed in the project's instructions. Fill in that pattern element; for circular elements, start in the center and work in a rough spiral; for lines, follow the contours of the design and do not try to follow the canvas grid exactly.

2 **Continue filling in pattern**
When working free-form, you may need to shift from one area of the canvas to the other. Carry the locking medium through the already-formed loops to the next hooking area, and carry the fabric or yarn across the back of the canvas under areas that have already been hooked.

3 **Surrounding design**
Continue filling in the design; when switching colors, continue to follow the contours of the pattern, surrounding the previously hooked areas with the new color. This will keep the design clear and defined.

Combining Methods

Combining locker hooking methods gives designs texture and movement. In the example shown here, the focal points of the design are created first with the free-form method to make them stand out from the design. The focal elements are further emphasized by filling in the background with linear locker hooking so the background doesn't distract from the rest of the design. Then a spiral border is used to frame the piece. Remember: there are no set rules about how to create a piece. When creating a design, try different methods to find which method or combination of methods works best with the design.

Additional Locker Hooking Techniques

Once you get comfortable with locker hooking basics, you can try some new techniques to enhance your designs. From adding textural elements to changing colors, try adding these techniques to your locker hooking repertoire.

Locker Hooking with Printed Fabrics

Printed fabrics are a great way to enhance your color palette for locker hooking. However, printed fabrics, just like a piece of paper coming out of a computer printer, have a right side—the printed side, which has a clear design—and a wrong side—the unprinted side, which is lighter in color and has an indistinct pattern. Unless you're going for a muted look, the wrong side must be hidden before you begin locker hooking.

1 Fold fabric
Cut or tear strips of printed fabric twice the width required for the project (see *Preparing Fabric*, page 18). Fold the strips in half widthwise with wrong sides together. Press with a hot iron if needed.

2 Locker hook
Locker hook as normal with the folded fabric strip (see *Basic Locker Hooking*, page 22).

Locker Hooking with Multiple Elements

I love using different elements together while locker hooking. It's a great way to create interesting textures. Fabric strips held together with a mohair or a blended yarn create a soft, touchable project. Combining ribbon with fabric strips or fibers can add a new dash of color or a more sophisticated look to a design. Try different combinations to find your favorites.

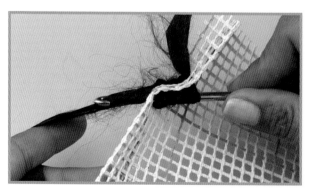

1 Combine elements
Align the elements you wish to use together and hold them together.

2 Locker hook
Locker hook as normal with the combined elements (see *Basic Locker Hooking*, page 22).

Attaching Additional Fabric

When working on a project, you often end up using many strips of fabric. You can easily attach another strip in a smooth bond when you reach the end of a strip and want to continue with the same color. Joining the strips together eliminates fabric or yarn tails and is useful for projects that require many strips of the same color or design, such as a rug.

1 Trim and align strips
Trim the exposed end of the old strip of fabric and 1 end of the new strip of fabric. Align the trimmed ends and hold the strips together.

2 Cut strips
Fold the strips over approximately 1" (3cm) from the ends. Snip ½" (1cm) through both fabric strips at the fold to create a 1" (3cm) slit.

3 Attach strips
Turn the new fabric strip around so that it faces the opposite direction and place it on top of the old strip. Overlap the slits cut in both strips of fabric. Bring the uncut end of the new strip up through the bottom of the slits in both strips.

4 Tighten connection
Pull the new strip of fabric through until there is no slack at the connection between the 2 strips. Continue locker hooking as normal (see *Basic Locker Hooking*, page 22).

Attaching Additional Locking Medium

Just as when you come to the end of a decorative strip and attach a new one, when you come to the end of your piece of locking medium, you need to attach a new piece.

1 Attach locking medium
To attach a new strand of locking medium, cut a new 2 yd. (2m) length of locking medium. For projects that receive lots of wear and tear, like rugs or bags, secure the locking medium by tying on additional string or yarn. Tie the new locking medium to the old locking medium with a double knot on the front of the work. For projects that don't receive a lot of wear and tear, you can add more and just leave a tail. Continue locker hooking as normal (see *Basic Locker Hooking*, page 22). The locking medium tails will get sewn in when the project is complete.

Switching Colors

Most locker hooking projects involve switching colors, sometimes several times. Luckily, switching colors is an easy process. Follow the steps below for a seamless transition in your design.

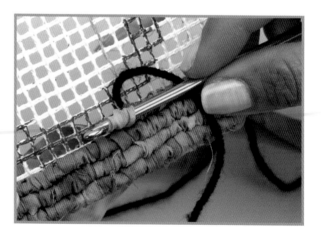

1 Start new strand
When you reach a point in the locker hooking design when a new color is added, allow the strip of fabric you were using to hang from the back of the canvas. Hold a fabric strip of the new color at the back of the canvas, push the locker hook through the next hole in the canvas and hook the new strip of fabric.

2 Continue working
Pull a loop of the new fabric up through the canvas leaving a 2" (5cm) tail at the back of the fabric. Continue locker hooking as usual (see *Basic Locker Hooking*, page 22).

Traveling Fabric Strips or Yarn

When working on a design, you may find that several portions of the design require the same color. You can travel your fabric strips across the back of the piece to the next section as long as you don't cover up any unhooked areas. Traveling many strips over the same area may add thickness to a design, so you should limit the amount of traveling you do over the same area so you don't end up with a bulky finished piece.

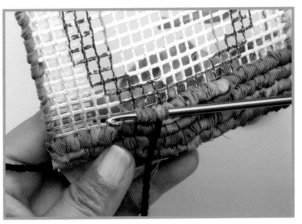

1 Arrange fabric

Locker hook as usual until you reach a point in the design where you switch back to a color you have already used (see *Basic Locker Hooking*, page 22). In this example, the design switched from pink to green and is switching back to pink. When you reach a point in the design where you start working with a color you have already used, pull the fabric strip in that color across the back of the work to the square where you will start working with it again. Make sure the strip lays flat on the back of the canvas and does not pass over any unhooked areas.

2 Continue working

Pull up a loop of the traveling fabric or yarn in the appropriate square. Continue locker hooking as usual.

Working in the Round

When creating a circular design like a basket, tote bag, lampshade or cuff bracelet, you'll be working in the round. Working in the round requires that you bring your canvas together to create a circle. Use clamps to hold your round design together if necessary.

1 Join canvas

Begin working the first row of the locker hooking pattern. Once you work up to approximately 1" (3cm) from the edge of the canvas, form the canvas into a circle and overlap the edges as indicated by your pattern. Place the hook through both pieces of canvas where they overlap, hook the fabric strip and pull up a loop through both pieces of canvas. Work through both pieces of canvas together across the overlapping areas on each row. Locker hooking through the overlapped section can often be a tight squeeze. This may require wriggling the hook gently until you pull through.

Finishing Techniques

Once you've finished locker hooking your pattern, you must complete the final steps to finish the piece. This includes sewing in all the tails to hide them. This step is especially important for any piece that requires a finished reverse side. I skip this step for pillow designs because the reverse side of the design is hidden when the pillow is sewn together. For a neat presentation, hide all tails, even if you put backing on flat pieces such as trivets, rugs, place mats or runners. This eliminates having a bulky reverse side.

Sewing in Fabric Tails

Sewing in fabric tails is easy but can take some time, depending on the number of tails. This step is worth the extra time, though, because it gives your piece a more polished look. This is where the length of your loops comes in to play: If you have some tight loops, you may have to wriggle your locker hook through them to sew in your tails. Use the needle eye end of the hook to make this process easier.

1 Trim tails
Once you have completed locker hooking the design, trim all the tails hanging from the back of the canvas to 1½–2" (4–5cm). Cut the strips on an angle, forming a point; this makes it easier to thread the strips through the eye of the locker hook.

2 Pull tail to front
Insert the eye of the locker hook through a hole in the canvas adjacent to the tail. Don't go through the same hole as the tail, or you will unravel your work. Thread the tail through the eye of the locker hook. Pull the tail to the front of the work.

3 Position locker hook
Starting 5 loops away from the tail, thread the eye of the locker hook through a row of loops, working toward the tail.

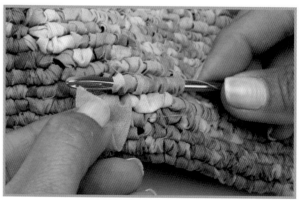

4 Position tail
Thread the tail through the eye of the locker hook.

5 **Hide tail**
Pull the tail through the loops on the locker hook.

6 **Trim tail**
Trim the tail close to the surface of the piece. Adjust the loops as needed to hide the tail.

Sewing in Locking Medium Tails

Sewing in the tails left by adding new pieces of locking medium is one more tidying up task to be done at the end of every project. Taking the time to sew in these ends not only makes your project look better, it also makes it more secure.

1 **Position locker hook**
Starting 5 loops away from the locking medium tail, thread the eye of the locker hook through a row of loops, working toward the tail. Thread the locking medium tail through the eye of the locker hook.

2 **Hide tail**
Pull the locking medium through the loops on the locker hook. Trim the locking medium tail close to the surface of the piece. Adjust the loops as needed to hide the locking medium tail.

Attaching Self-Adhesive Fabric Lining

Using a self-adhesive fabric lining is a quick and easy way to neatly cover the back of any locker hooked project. Not only is the lining attractive, but it also protects the back of your piece from snags, wear and tear. This type of lining is only good for projects that won't be washed, however, because the adhesive is water-soluble. To make this lining waterproof, add a line of fast-drying permanent adhesive around the edge of the lining.

1 Cut fabric
Outline the shape of the finished project on the self-adhesive fabric. Mark a corner on your project and the back of the sheet so you can anchor the backing exactly where you traced it and have a good fit. Cut along the marked lines.

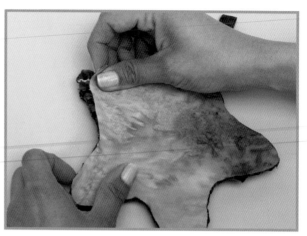

2 Attach lining
Peel the protective paper off of the fabric. Align the fabric with the locker hooked piece carefully and press the adhesive side of the fabric firmly to the back of the piece.

Sewing on Fabric

For projects that will be washed, a hand-stitched lining or backing is the best choice. This method takes some time, but it is the perfect finishing touch for a beautifully finished project.

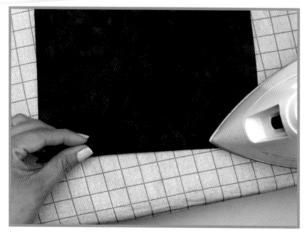

1 Prepare fabric
Measure and cut the lining fabric, adding the seam allowance required for the project. Use the seam allowance to adjust for a perfect fit by pressing it back according to the measurements of your project.

2 Attach lining
Using a slip stitch, sew the lining fabric to the yarn or fabric used to frame the piece. Use small stitches for a neat appearance.

Assembling a Project

Assembling a locker hooked project has traditionally been reserved for piecing rugs together, but the projects in this book go so much further than just rugs! You can create unique locker hooked pieces by making several small pieces and then assembling them into a basket, bag and more.

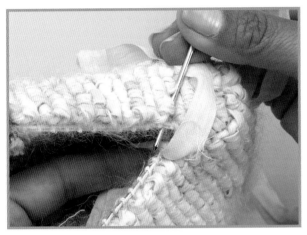

1 Prepare pieces
Align the two locker hooked pieces for sewing. Thread a tapestry needle with a strip of fabric that matches the project. Thread the needle through the exposed canvas at the edge of one of the pieces.

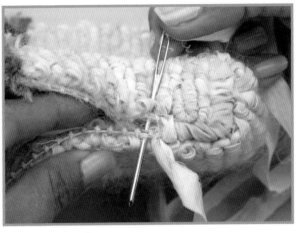

2 Begin sewing
Thread the needle through a square at the edge of the second piece of canvas diagonal to the square on the first piece of canvas.

3 Cover raw edges
Pull the fabric strip through both pieces until it is snug; arrange the fabric strip so that it lays neatly and completely covers the canvas edge.

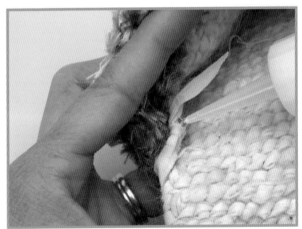

4 Secure knot
Work the entire seam. When it is complete, tie the fabric strip in an overhand knot. Secure the knot with a drop of glue.

home decor

W hile locker hooking has primarily been used for rug making, there are many home decor items that can be locker hooked. Pillows, place mats, table runners, coasters and trivets, even lampshades, are all great candidates for a locker hooked design. And while locker hooking may seem to have an inherent homespun, country feel, you can also create more modern and elegant pieces—even ultra-hip designs—that work well with a variety of interior designs. A locker hooked project can add a special touch to any style of home decor.

Try one of my pillow designs, like the *Safari Pillow* on page 57 or the *Cabbage Rose Pillow* on page 69, for a comfortable and chic addition to your couch or bed. Or, make your own pillow design and combine fibers and fabrics to fit your own style. A locker hooked rug, like the *Wild Colors Rug* on page 44, is a great accent piece and can be customized with different colors, or even a different size, to fit into any design scheme. Locker hooking is endlessly customizable. Use colors that match your interior decor or add texture by varying the loop lengths and mixing different fibers. The choices are all up to you!

And while many locker hooked items are both functional and beautiful, like the *Garden Trivet Trio* on page 60, you can just focus on looks alone. Go crazy with beads, buttons and other embellishments to create your own locker hooked piece of art, like the *Home Blessing Wall Hanging* on page 75. When it comes to locker hooking, the only limit is your imagination.

Candy Stripe Coasters

THERESA PULIDO

These coasters are a great first project because they are super-simple but also cute and fun. I came up with this design because I wanted something festive for an outdoor summer bash that I could whip up quickly. The idea of these easy-to-make coasters with stripes was hard to resist. The striped design is reminiscent of a candy cane or striped mint candies. Follow the charts on page 38, or alter the width of the stripes in each coaster to make them all unique. Try different colors, too—orange, green, pink or purple would all look wonderful in this pattern. The red, white and blue are classic choices for summer. For more striped fun, enlarge the size and make a trivet or place mat to match your coasters.

materials

Size 5 rug canvas

19 yd. (17.5m) red fabric strips, cut to ½" (13mm) for batik fabrics or ¾" (2cm) for printed fabrics

19 yd. (17.5m) blue fabric strips, cut to ½" (13mm) for batik fabrics or ¾" (2cm) for printed fabrics

30 yd. (27.5m) white or ivory fabric strips, cut to ½" (13mm) for batik fabrics or ¾" (2cm) for printed fabrics

Locking medium

Locker hook

Tapestry needle

Scissors

Permanent markers

1 **Prepare base**
Cut a piece of rug canvas that measures 26 squares wide and 26 squares tall for each coaster (see *Preparing the Base*, page 19). Fold under 2 squares of canvas on each edge of each piece of canvas (see *Securing the Edges of the Base*, pages 20–21). Mark the patterns from page 38 on the pieces of canvas.

2 **Frame canvas**
Frame each piece of canvas in red or blue fabric to match the color you've chosen for the stripes (see *Framing the Canvas*, page 21).

3 **Locker hook pattern**
Begin locker hooking, following the charts on page 38 or the patterns you've marked on the pieces of canvas (see *Basic Locker Hooking*, page 22). Start in the bottom right corner of the coaster and work using the linear method of locker hooking (see *Linear Locker Hooking*, page 24).

4 **Finish coaster**
Once the locker hooking is complete, sew in the fabric tail ends and the locking medium ends (see *Finishing Techniques*, pages 30–31).

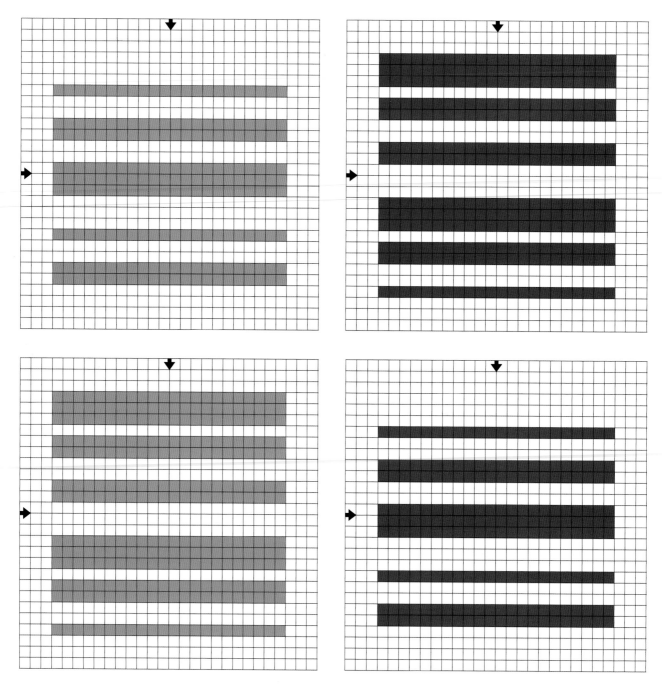

Candy Stripe Coasters

Geometry Place Mats

KATHLEEN CARPENTER

These place mats are simple but striking with their black-and-white color palette. I love this look for a modern table setting. Add a simple, contemporary dinnerware setting and you've got a great look. And, of course, black and white go with everything! The pattern for these place mats is a generously large size, but if you need the space and want to reduce the size, you can take off some of the width and they'll still work well. If you like symmetry, you can choose just one of these patterns and make a matching set, or for a more freewheeling look for your table, combine the two patterns in a set.

materials

Size 5 rug canvas

275 yd. (251.5m) black fabric strips,
cut to ½" (13mm) for batik fabrics
or ¾" (2cm) for printed fabrics

50 yd. (46m) white or ivory fabric strips,
cut to ½" (13mm) for batik fabrics or
¾" (2cm) for printed fabrics

Locking medium

Locker hook

Tapestry needle

Scissors

Permanent markers

1 Prepare base
Cut a piece of rug canvas that measures 102 squares wide and 71 squares tall for each place mat (see *Preparing the Base*, page 19). Fold under 3 squares of canvas on each edge (see *Securing the Edge of the Base*, pages 20–21). Mark the patterns from page 41 on the pieces of canvas.

2 Frame canvas
Frame the pieces of canvas with black or white fabric (see *Framing the Canvas*, page 21). For my place mats, I framed one in black fabric and one in white.

3 Locker hook pattern
Begin locker hooking, following the charts on page 41 or the patterns you've marked on the pieces of canvas (see *Basic Locker Hooking*, page 22). Start in the bottom right corner of the place mat and work using the linear method of locker hooking (see *Linear Locker Hooking*, page 24).

4 Finish place mats
Once the locker hooking is complete, sew in the fabric tail ends and the locking medium ends (see *Finishing Techniques*, pages 30–31).

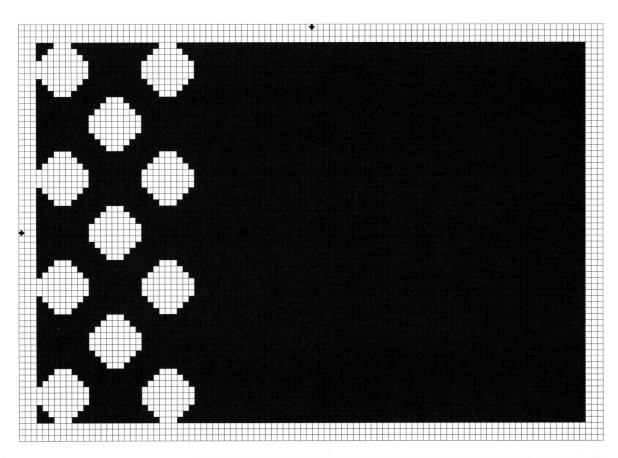

Geometry Place Mats

Circles-in-Circles Coasters

THERESA PULIDO

For this set of coasters, I wanted to create a simple design with a modern appeal and decided to try circles. This simple, graphic design provides a burst of bright colors for any setting. They're perfect for a patio setting and fun for an outdoor party, especially one with a tropical theme. You can make all your coasters the same or mix it up with several different colors. Color coordinate these coasters with your tumblers or cocktail glasses for a fun look.

materials

Size 5 rug canvas

39 yd. (36m) green fabric strips, cut to ½" (13mm) for batik fabrics or ¾" (2cm) for printed fabrics

30 yd. (27.5m) blue fabric strips, cut to ½" (13mm) for batik fabrics or ¾" (2cm) for printed fabrics

24 yd. (22m) pink fabric strips, cut to ½" (13mm) for batik fabrics or ¾" (2cm) for printed fabrics

15 yd. (14m) orange fabric strips, cut to ½" (13mm) for batik fabrics or ¾" (2cm) for printed fabrics

Locking medium

Locker hook

Tapestry needle

Scissors

Permanent markers

1 Prepare base
Cut a piece of rug canvas that measures 28 squares wide and 28 squares tall for each coaster (see *Preparing the Base*, page 19). Fold under 2 squares of canvas on each edge (see *Securing the Edges of the Base*, pages 20–21). Mark the pattern below on each piece of canvas.

2 Frame canvas
Frame each piece of canvas with the fabric you plan to use for the center circle of the coaster (see *Framing the Canvas*, page 21).

3 Locker hook pattern
Begin locker hooking, following the chart below or the pattern you've marked on the pieces of canvas (see *Basic Locker Hooking*, page 22). Start in the bottom right corner of the coaster and work using the linear method of locker hooking, switching colors as needed to follow the pattern (see *Linear Locker Hooking*, page 24, and *Switching Colors*, page 28). To avoid a bulky coaster, only travel the fabric strips at the top and bottom of the circle (see *Traveling Fabric Strips or Yarn*, page 29).

4 Finish coaster
Once the locker hooking is complete, sew in the fabric tail ends and the locking medium ends (see *Finishing Techniques*, pages 30–31).

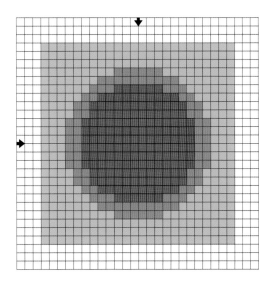

Wild Colors Rug

KATHLEEN CARPENTER

*M*aking this wild rug is a great way to use up leftover yardage from your fabric stash. The beauty of this design lies in its simplicity and flexibility. You can alter the size to make something as small as a coaster, make just one square to use as a trivet, or follow the pattern to make a beautiful rug. You can also continue to add squares until you have a larger rug or a long runner. Customize the colors to suit your decor, or mix it up with all the colors in the rainbow. To make all your crazy colors come together, use a unifying color to outline each square and you're sure to have a knockout project.

materials

Size 3.75 rug canvas

100 yd. (91.5m) black-and-white patterned fabric strips, cut to ¾" (2cm) for batik fabrics or 1" (3cm) for printed fabrics

55 yd. (50.5m) fabric strips in a solid color, cut to ¾" (2cm) for batik fabrics or 1" (3cm) for printed fabrics

220 yd. (201.5m) fabric strips in a variety of colors, cut to ¾" (2cm) for batik fabrics or 1" (3cm) for printed fabrics

Locking medium

Locker hook

Tapestry needle

Scissors

Sewing machine and thread

1 Prepare base
Cut 6 pieces of rug canvas that measure 42 squares wide and 42 squares tall (see *Preparing the Base*, page 19). Fold under 3 squares of canvas on each edge and secure the edge by stitching it (see *Securing the Edges of the Base*, pages 20–21).

2 Locker hook pattern
Begin locker hooking, following the chart on page 46 (see *Basic Locker Hooking*, page 22). Start at the center of each square and work using the spiral method of locker hooking (see *Spiral Locker Hooking*, page 24).

3 Assemble squares
When all the squares have been locker hooked, sew the squares together in a 2 × 3 pattern using black-and-white fabric strips (see *Assembling a Project*, page 33).

4 Finish rug
Frame the outer edge of the rug with black-and-white fabric strips (see *Framing the Canvas*, page 21). Sew in the fabric tail ends and the locking medium ends (see *Finishing Techniques*, pages 30–31).

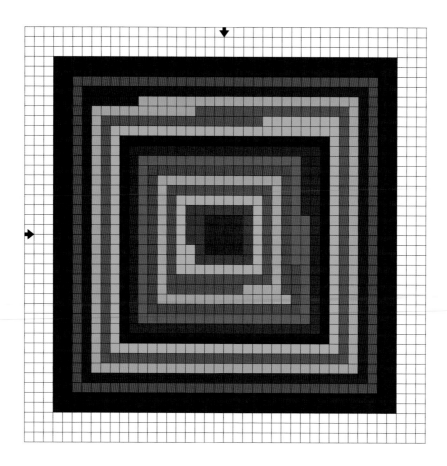

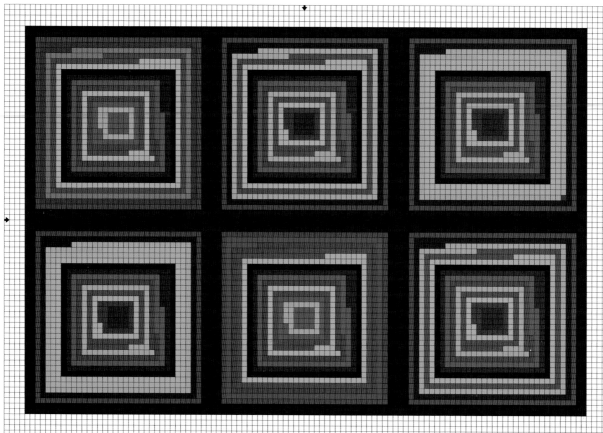

Wild Colors Rug

Checkers and Dots Centerpiece

KATHLEEN CARPENTER

This stylish centerpiece has a modern look that can complement a dinner table or a cocktail table. In black and white, this pattern composed of squares and circles is striking, but try different color combinations for a new look. Orange and red would complement decor with a warm color palette, while a combination of pastels would lend a dreamy look to this project. Turning this centerpiece into a table runner is quick and easy—simply double the length of the piece to run the full length of the table. For matching place mats, shorten the pattern and you can have a beautifully coordinated table.

materials

Size 5 rug canvas

145 yd. (133m) black fabric strips, cut to ½" (13mm) for batik fabrics or ¾" (2cm) for printed fabrics

195 yd. (178.5m) white or ivory fabric strips, cut to ½" (13mm) for batik fabrics or ¾" (2cm) for printed fabrics

Locking medium

Locker hook

Tapestry needle

Scissors

Permanent markers

1 Prepare base
Cut a piece of rug canvas that measures 71 squares wide and 155 squares tall (see *Preparing the Base*, page 19). Fold under 3 squares of canvas on each edge (see *Securing the Edges of the Base*, pages 20–21). Mark the pattern from page 49 on the piece of canvas.

2 Frame canvas
Frame the piece of canvas with black fabric (see *Framing the Canvas*, page 21).

3 Locker hook pattern
Begin locker hooking, following the chart on page 49 or the pattern you've marked on the canvas (see *Basic Locker Hooking*, page 22). Start in the bottom right corner of the centerpiece and work using the linear method of locker hooking (see *Linear Locker Hooking*, page 24).

4 Finish centerpiece
Once the locker hooking is complete, sew in the fabric tail ends and the locking medium ends (see *Finishing Techniques*, pages 30–31).

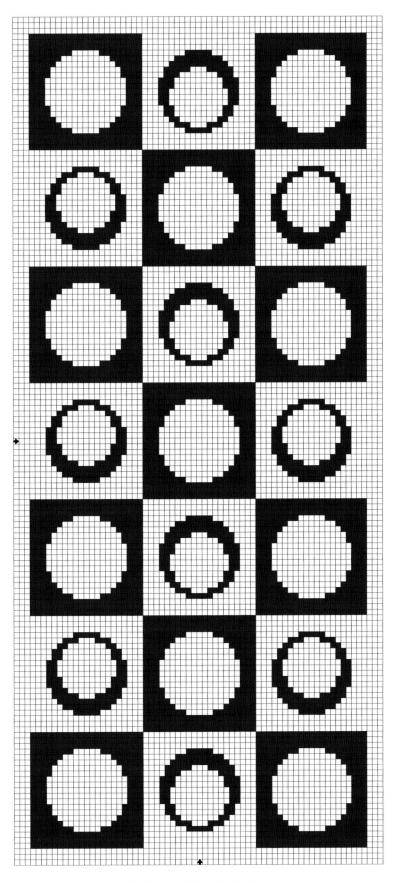

Checkers and Dots Centerpiece

Welcoming Mat

KATHLEEN CARPENTER

*I*f you've ever wondered what you could do with that collection of plastic bags, here's a unique way to recycle them and create a great-looking rug at the same time. Instead of ending up in a landfill, used plastic bags can be part of a friendly welcome for guests. And don't be afraid to put it outside your door—this tough rug stands up to wear and tear and can easily be washed and drip dried. Choose your own colors to customize the look.

materials

Size 3.75 rug canvas

423 white 2"-wide (5cm) plastic bag rings

321 black 2"-wide (5cm) plastic bag rings

18 red 2"-wide (5cm) plastic bag rings

18 green 2"-wide (5cm) plastic bag rings

12 purple 2"-wide (5cm) plastic bag rings

6 turquoise 2"-wide (5cm) plastic bag rings

6 pink 2"-wide (5cm) plastic bag rings

6 orange 2"-wide (5cm) plastic bag rings

3 yellow 2"-wide (5cm) plastic bag rings

Locking medium

Locker hook

Tapestry needle

Scissors

Permanent markers

Sewing machine and thread

1 Prepare base

Cut a piece of rug canvas that measures 126 squares wide and 78 squares tall (see *Preparing the Base*, page 19). Cut off the bottom left and right corners of the piece of canvas. Fold under 3 squares of canvas on each edge and secure the edge by stitching it with a sewing machine (see *Securing the Edges of the Base*, pages 20–21). Mark the pattern from page 53 on the canvas. See page 52 for instructions on preparing the plastic strips for locker hooking.

2 Frame canvas

Frame the pieces of canvas with black plastic strips (see *Framing the Canvas*, page 21).

3 Locker hook pattern

Begin locker hooking, following the chart on page 53 or the pattern you've marked on the canvas (see *Basic Locker Hooking*, page 22). Start in the top right corner of the mat and work using the linear method of locker hooking (see *Linear Locker Hooking*, page 24).

4 Finish mat

Once the locker hooking is complete, sew in the plastic tail ends and the locking medium ends (see *Finishing Techniques*, pages 30–31).

Creating Plastic Rings

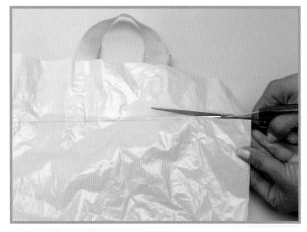

1 Begin cutting
Remove the handle and any double-thickness or reinforced areas from the bag.

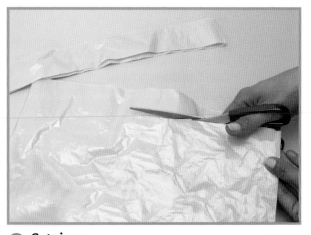

2 Cut rings
Cut the remainder of the bag into rings that are 2" (5cm) wide.

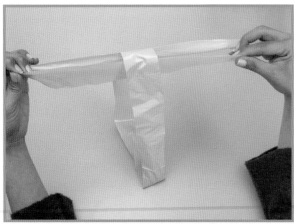

3 Start join
To join rings into a continuous length, slide 1 ring through another.

4 Continue join
Bring one end of the ring in your hands through the other end of the same ring.

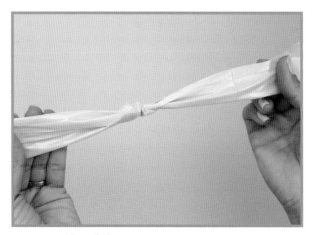

5 Complete join
Pull both rings in opposite directions to close the connection.

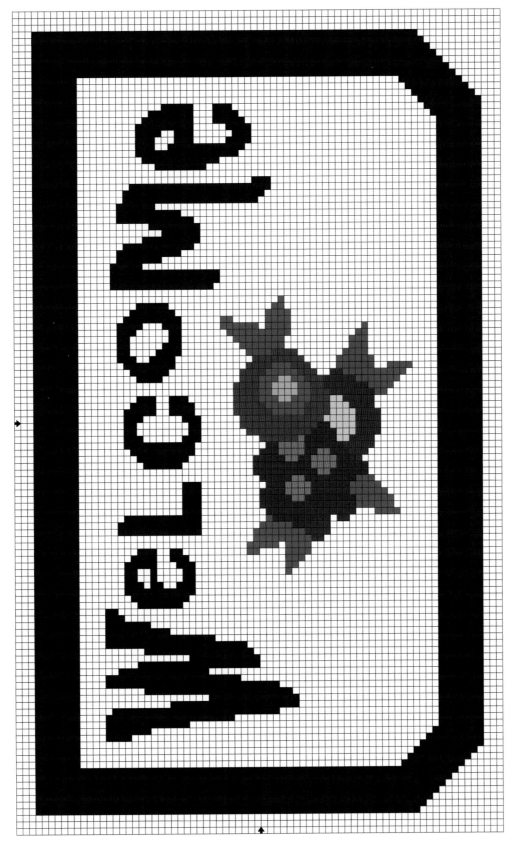

Welcoming Mat

Woolen Coasters

KATHLEEN CARPENTER

*G*ive wool yarn a try in this locker hooked project! This set of wool coasters has a great geometric design, and the wool gives it a wonderfully fuzzy texture. This design would also look great if made with fabric strips instead of wool yarn. Either way, this is a great design that allows you to play with color choice. For a matching set, make the base color the same for all the coasters and have fun playing with the accent colors.

materials

Size 5 rug canvas

22 yd. (20.5m) blue 3-ply wool yarn

20 yd. (18.5m) green 3-ply wool yarn

19 yd. (17.5m) yellow 3-ply wool yarn

21 yd. (19.5m) orange 3-ply wool yarn

Locking medium

Locker hook

Tapestry needle

Scissors

Permanent markers

1 **Prepare base**
Cut a piece of rug canvas that measures 29 squares wide and 29 squares tall for each coaster (see *Preparing the Base*, page 19). Fold under 2 squares of canvas on each edge of each piece of canvas (see *Securing the Edges of the Base*, pages 20–21). Mark the patterns from page 56 on the pieces of canvas.

2 **Frame canvas**
Frame each piece of canvas with yarn that is the main color for the pattern you've chosen (see *Framing the Canvas*, page 21).

3 **Locker hook pattern**
Begin locker hooking, following the charts on page 56 or the patterns you've marked on the pieces of canvas (see *Basic Locker Hooking*, page 22). Start in the bottom right corner of the coaster and work using the linear method of locker hooking (see *Linear Locker Hooking*, page 24).

4 **Finish coaster**
Once the locker hooking is complete, sew in the yarn ends and the locking medium ends (see *Finishing Techniques*, pages 30–31).

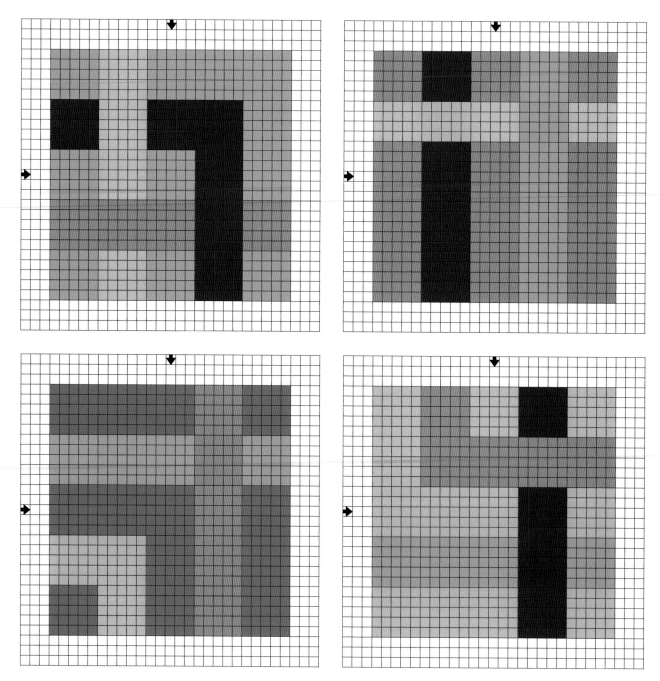

Woolen Coasters

Safari Pillow

THERESA PULIDO

*T*he wonderful pre-cut wool strips I used in this project were the perfect texture for this rich, nature-inspired design. This design was a tough one to finish—it took me a few tries to get the zebra design just right, but it was so rewarding to finally see it stuffed and finished. The wool strips I used are only available in two-yard lengths, so I had to use quite a few pieces, which meant quite a few tails. However, because a backing is sewn onto this piece to create a pillow, the tails will remain tucked away without a lot of tedious sewing in. This rectangular design makes a beautiful accent pillow for a chair or a great centerpiece among a variety of other pillows on a bed or sofa. Substitute ½" (13mm) fabric strips in this pattern if you can't find wool strips.

materials

Size 5 rug canvas

60 yd. (55m) cream wool fabric strips, cut to ¼" (6mm)

40 yd. (37m) brown wool fabric strips, cut to ¼" (6mm)

Locking medium

Locker hook

Tapestry needle

Scissors

Permanent markers

Needle and thread

Iron

15" × 10" (38cm × 25cm) piece of cloth that coordinates with the wool strips

14" × 8½" (36cm × 22cm) pillow form

1 Prepare base
Cut a piece of rug canvas that measures 78 squares wide and 53 squares tall (see *Preparing the Base*, page 19). Fold under 3 squares of canvas on each edge (see *Securing the Edges of the Base*, pages 20–21). Mark the pattern from page 59 on the canvas.

2 Frame canvas
Frame the canvas with brown wool fabric strips (see *Framing the Canvas*, page 21).

3 Locker hook pattern
Begin locker hooking, following the chart on page 59 or the pattern you've marked on the canvas (see *Basic Locker Hooking*, page 22). Start with the brown stripes and work using the free-form method of locker hooking (see *Free-Form Locker Hooking*, page 25). After the brown stripes are complete, locker hook the cream stripes using the free-form method.

4 Assemble pillow
Fold over a ½" (13mm) seam allowance on each side of the coordinating fabric and steam press down. Measure the fabric against the locker hooked piece; adjust the fabric to match and steam press any adjustments. Slip stitch the fabric to the locker hooked piece on 3 sides. Insert the pillow form. Slip stitch the last side to finish the pillow.

Safari Pillow

I love cooking and entertaining. Somehow, parties always end up in the kitchen, so I wanted to design something that could be useful in the kitchen but would also make great wall art when not in use. I came up with these trivets that serve a useful purpose while adding a nice decorative touch to any kitchen. You can hang them on the wall and pull them down as needed or leave them on the counter. If you're preparing something to share with guests, they'll come in handy under a hot dish or sauté pan. They're also perfect on the table for a casual lunch or dinner. Make one or all three, for a great project you'll use and enjoy.

materials

PEPPERS

Size 5 rug canvas

38 yd. (35m) yellow fabric strips, cut to ½" (13mm) for batik fabrics or ¾" (2cm) for printed fabrics

24 yd. (22m) green fabric strips, cut to ½" (13mm) for batik fabrics or ¾" (2cm) for printed fabrics

8 yd. (7.5m) red fabric strips, cut to ½" (13mm) for batik fabrics or ¾" (2cm) for printed fabrics

2 yd. (2m) bright green fabric strips, cut to ½" (13mm) for batik fabrics or ¾" (2cm) for printed fabrics

1 yd. (1m) dark green fabric strips, cut to ½" (13mm) for batik fabrics or ¾" (2cm) for printed fabrics

Locking medium

Locker hook

Tapestry needle

Scissors

Permanent markers

GARLIC

Size 5 rug canvas

30 yd. (27.5m) yellow fabric strips, cut to ½" (13mm) for batik fabrics or ¾" (2cm) for printed fabrics

16 yd. (15m) green fabric strips, cut to ½" (13mm) for batik fabrics or ¾" (2cm) for printed fabrics

20 yd. (18.5m) white fabric strips, cut to ½" (13mm) for batik fabrics or ¾" (2cm) for printed fabrics

6 yd. (5.5m) brown fabric strips, cut to ½" (13mm) for batik fabrics or ¾" (2cm) for printed fabrics

Locking medium

Locker hook

Tapestry needle

Scissors

Permanent markers

ARTICHOKE

Size 5 rug canvas

20 yd. (18.5m) yellow fabric strips, cut to ½" (13mm) for batik fabrics or ¾" (2cm) for printed fabrics

16 yd. (15m) green fabric strips, cut to ½" (13mm) for batik fabrics or ¾" (2cm) for printed fabrics

30 yd. (27.5m) bright green fabric strips, cut to ½" (13mm) for batik fabrics or ¾" (2cm) for printed fabrics

8 yd. (7.5m) dark green fabric strips, cut to ½" (13mm) for batik fabrics or ¾" (2cm) for printed fabrics

Locking medium

Locker hook

Tapestry needle

Scissors

Permanent markers

Peppers

1 Prepare base
Cut a piece of rug canvas that measures 48 squares wide and 54 squares tall (see *Preparing the Base*, page 19). Fold under 3 squares of canvas on each edge (see *Securing the Edges of the Base*, pages 20–21). Mark the pattern below on the canvas.

2 Frame canvas
Frame the canvas with green fabric strips (see *Framing the Canvas*, page 21).

3 Locker hook pattern
Begin locker hooking, following the chart below or the pattern you've marked on the canvas (see *Basic Locker Hooking*, page 22). Start with the border and work using the spiral method of locker hooking (see *Spiral Locker Hooking*, page 24). Next, fill in the peppers using the free-form method of locker hooking (see *Free-Form Locker Hooking*, page 25). Finally, work the background using the linear method of locker hooking (see *Linear Locker Hooking*, page 24).

4 Finish trivet
Once the locker hooking is complete, sew in the fabric tail ends and the locking medium ends (see *Finishing Techniques*, pages 30–31).

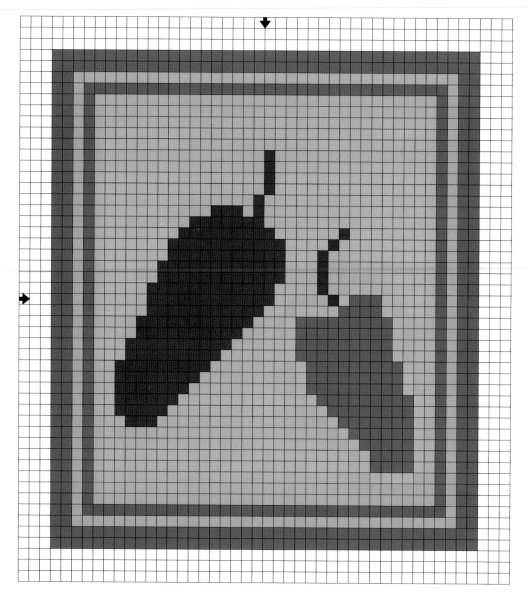

Peppers Garden Trivet

Garlic

1 Prepare base

Cut a piece of rug canvas that measures 48 squares wide and 54 squares tall (see *Preparing the Base*, page 19). Fold under 3 squares of canvas on each edge (see *Securing the Edges of the Base*, pages 20–21). Mark the pattern below on the canvas.

2 Frame canvas

Frame the canvas with green fabric strips (see *Framing the Canvas*, page 21).

3 Locker hook pattern

Begin locker hooking, following the chart below or the pattern you've marked on the canvas

(see *Basic Locker Hooking*, page 22). Start with the border and work using the spiral method of locker hooking (see *Spiral Locker Hooking*, page 24). Once the border is complete, start in the bottom right corner inside the border and complete the design using the linear method of locker hooking, switching colors as needed to follow the pattern (see *Linear Locker Hooking*, page 24, and *Switching Colors*, page 28).

4 Finish trivet

Once the locker hooking is complete, sew in the fabric tail ends and the locking medium ends (see *Finishing Techniques*, pages 30–31).

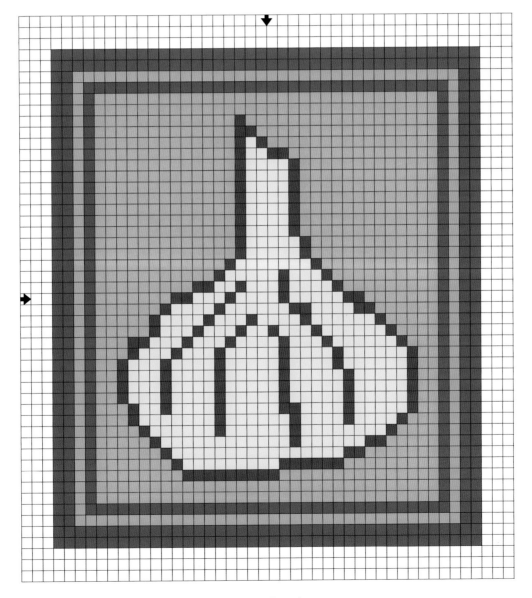

Garlic Garden Trivet

Artichoke

1 Prepare base
Cut a piece of rug canvas that measures 48 squares wide and 54 squares tall (see *Preparing the Base*, page 19). Fold under 3 squares of canvas on each edge (see *Securing the Edges of the Base*, pages 20–21). Mark the pattern below on the canvas.

2 Frame canvas
Frame the canvas with green fabric strips (see *Framing the Canvas*, page 21).

3 Locker hook pattern
Begin locker hooking, following the chart below or the pattern you've marked on the canvas (see *Basic Locker Hooking*, page 22). Start with the border and work using the spiral method of locker hooking (see *Spiral Locker Hooking*, page 24). Once the border is complete, start in the bottom right corner inside the border and complete the design using the linear method of locker hooking, switching colors to follow the pattern (see *Linear Locker Hooking*, page 24, and *Switching Colors*, page 28).

4 Finish trivet
Once the locker hooking is complete, sew in the fabric tail ends and the locking medium ends (see *Finishing Techniques*, pages 30–31).

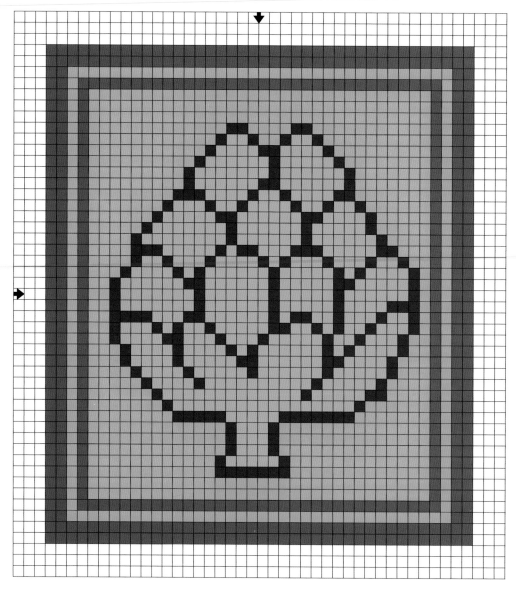

Artichoke Garden Trivet

Lovely Luminaries

THERESA PULIDO

I was so excited when I discovered the lamp-making kit I used in this project because I thought it would be fantastic for a locker hooking project. You can create these lamps to match your own style and fit a room—hip and trendy, beaded boudoir, simple and modern—the choice is yours. The first lamp I made took on a very hip 1970s look because of the resin beads at the bottom. You can enhance the funkiness of this design by pulling up big loops for added dimension. Using the silk strips on the second lamp created a richer, more elegant look. As you can see, it's easy to make these lamps into whatever you want them to be. Add fringe, beads or other embellishments to further personalize your own project.

materials

LARGE LAMP

Size 3.75 rug canvas

38 yd. (35m) turquoise fabric strips, cut to ¾" (2cm) for batik fabrics or 1" (3cm) for printed fabrics

16 yd. (15m) bright turquoise flannel fabric strips, cut to ½" (13mm) for batik fabrics or 1" (3cm) for printed fabrics

32 yd. (29.5m) blue-green flannel fabric strips, cut to ½" (13mm) for batik fabrics or 1" (3cm) for printed fabrics

2 yd. (2m) lime green yarn or batik fabric strips cut to ¼" (6mm) to attach beads

Locking medium

Locker hook

Tapestry needle

Scissors

Clamps

Luminary kit

Green fabric paint

Paintbrush

12 5mm square yellow crystal beads

6 7mm round green ceramic beads

6 9mm blue glass pony beads

6 40mm lime green resin donut beads

6 40mm green resin donut beads

SMALL LAMP

Size 3.75 rug canvas

60 yd. (55m) magenta silk fabric strips, cut to ½" (13mm)

2½ yd. (2.5m) magenta beading thread or silk fabric strips cut to ¼" (6mm) to attach beads

Locking medium

Locker hook

Tapestry needle

Scissors

Clamps

Luminary kit

12 4mm square red crystal beads

12 7mm round red glass beads

12 18mm round red resin beads

Large Lamp

1 Prepare base
Cut a piece of rug canvas that measures 87 squares wide and 46 squares tall (see *Preparing the Base*, page 19). Paint the canvas with green fabric paint. Allow the paint to dry completely. Fold under 3 squares of canvas on the top edge of the canvas (see *Securing the Edges of the Base*, pages 20–21). Work the canvas around the top ring of the luminary kit as shown on page 68. Clamp the canvas to hold it in place.

2 Frame top edge of canvas
Frame the top edge of the lamp with turquoise fabric strips (see *Framing the Canvas*, page 21). Catch the metal ring inside the canvas with your stitching as shown on page 68. This will hold the ring in place. Work only the top edge. The bottom will be framed later.

3 Locker hook pattern
Starting at the top edge, begin locker hooking, following the chart on page 68 (see *Basic Locker Hooking*, page 22). Work using the linear method of locker hooking (see *Linear Locker Hooking*, page 24).

4 Frame bottom edge of canvas
Fold under 3 squares of canvas on the bottom edge of the canvas, working the canvas around the bottom ring from the luminary kit. Frame the bottom edge of the lamp with turquoise fabric strips, catching the metal ring inside the canvas with your stitching. Sew in the fabric tail ends and the locking medium ends (see *Finishing Techniques*, pages 30–31). Secure the lampshade to the base following the manufacturer's instructions.

5 Attach beads
Cut the lime green yarn or fabric strips into 12 6" (15cm) pieces. Knot the end of each strip. On 6 strips, string 1 lime green donut bead, 1 blue glass pony bead and 1 square yellow crystal bead. On the remaining 6 strips, string 1 green donut bead, 1 green ceramic bead and 1 square yellow crystal bead. Sew the beaded strips to the bottom of the lamp, spacing them equally around the lamp and alternating colors.

Small Lamp

1 Prepare base
Cut a piece of rug canvas that measures 64 squares wide and 41 squares tall (see *Preparing the Base*, page 19). Fold under 3 squares of canvas on the top edge of the canvas (see *Securing the Edges of the Base*, pages 20–21). Work the canvas around the top ring of the luminary kit as shown on page 68. Clamp the canvas to hold it in a circle.

2 Frame top edge of canvas
Frame the top edge of the lamp with magenta silk fabric strips (see *Framing the Canvas*, page 21). Catch the metal ring inside the canvas with your stitching as shown on page 68. This will hold the ring in place. Work only the top edge. The bottom will be framed later.

3 Locker hook pattern
Starting at the top edge, begin locker hooking, working the entire canvas with magenta silk strips (see *Basic Locker Hooking*, page 22). Work using the linear method of locker hooking (see *Linear Locker Hooking*, page 24). Stop locker hooking 4 rows from the bottom of the canvas.

4 Frame bottom edge of canvas
Fold under 3 squares of canvas on the bottom edge of the canvas, working the canvas around the bottom ring from the luminary kit. Frame the bottom of the lamp with magenta silk fabric strips, catching the metal ring inside the canvas with your stitching. Sew in the fabric tail ends and the locking medium ends (see *Finishing Techniques*, pages 30–31). Secure the lampshade to the lamp following the manufacturer's instructions.

5 Attach beads
Cut 12 7" (18cm) pieces of magenta beading thread or silk. Knot the end of each strand and string 1 resin bead, 1 round glass bead and 1 square crystal bead on each strip. Sew the beaded strips to the bottom of the lamp, spacing them equally around the lamp.

Attaching Canvas to the Lamp Frame

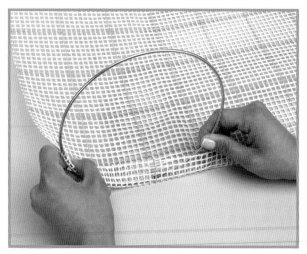 

1 Insert ring
Fold under the edge of the canvas. Wrap the canvas around the metal ring, with the ring inside the fold.

2 Secure ring
Clamp the canvas to hold it around the ring. Frame the folded edge of the canvas with fabric strips (see *Framing the Canvas*, page 21). Catch the metal ring inside the canvas with your stitching.

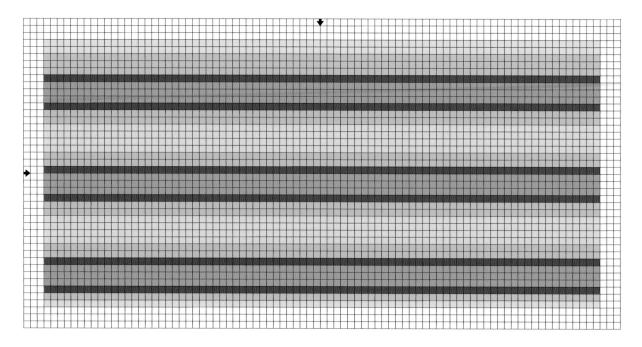

Lovely Luminaries

Cabbage Rose Pillow

THERESA PULIDO

This floral motif is created with a combination of materials including silk, wool and mohair for a rich, luxurious look. A beautiful silk backing completes this sumptuous project. Although this pillow is not as easy to make as some of the other projects in this book, it is well worth the extra effort. The delicate, feminine colors used in this example give the pillow a vintage look. Bold, modern colors can be used to bring this project up-to-date. No matter what the color palette, the different textures used in this pillow make it warm and welcoming.

materials

Size 5 rug canvas

16 yd. (15m) green wool fabric strips, cut to ¼" (6mm)

16 yd. (15m) magenta wool fabric strips, cut to ¼" (6mm)

10 yd. (9.5m) green silk fabric strips, cut to ½" (13mm)

12 yd. (11m) magenta silk fabric strips, cut to ½" (13mm)

24 yd. (22m) green fabric strips, cut to ½" (13mm) for batik fabrics or ¾" (2cm) for printed fabrics

10 yd. (9.5m) pink fabric strips, cut to ½" (13mm) for batik fabrics or ¾" (2cm) for printed fabrics

40 yd. (37m) white or cream fabric strips, cut to ½" (13mm) for batik fabrics or ¾" (2cm) for printed fabrics

25 yd. (23m) white mohair yarn

Locking medium

Locker hook

Tapestry needle

Scissors

Permanent markers

Needle and thread

Iron

13½" × 13½" (34cm × 34cm) piece of silk or satin cloth that coordinates with the fabric strips

13" × 13" (33cm × 33cm) pillow form

1 Prepare base
Cut a piece of rug canvas that measures 72 squares wide and 72 squares tall (see *Preparing the Base*, page 19). Fold under 2 squares of canvas on each edge (see *Securing the Edges of the Base*, pages 20–21). Mark the pattern from page 71 on the canvas.

2 Frame canvas
Frame the canvas with white or cream fabric strips (see *Framing the Canvas*, page 21).

3 Locker hook pattern
Begin locker hooking, following the chart on page 71 or the pattern you've marked on the canvas (see *Basic Locker Hooking*, page 22). Start with the magenta silk outline of the flower and work using the free-form method of locker hooking (see *Free-Form Locker Hooking*, page 25). Fill in the flower with pink and white or cream fabric strips using the free-form method. Next, locker hook the outline of the leaves with green silk strips. Fill in the leaves with green wool strips and green fabric strips. Locker hook the background, working in the spiral method of locker hooking (see *Spiral Locker Hooking*, page 24). Use magenta wool strips and white or cream fabric strips held together with mohair yarn to complete the background (see *Locker Hooking with Multiple Elements*, page 26).

4 Assemble pillow
Fold over a ½" (13mm) seam allowance on each side of the coordinating silk or satin fabric and steam press down. Measure the fabric against the locker hooked piece; adjust the fabric to match and steam press any adjustments. Slip stitch the fabric to the locker hooked piece on 3 sides. Insert the pillow form. Slip stitch the last side to finish the pillow.

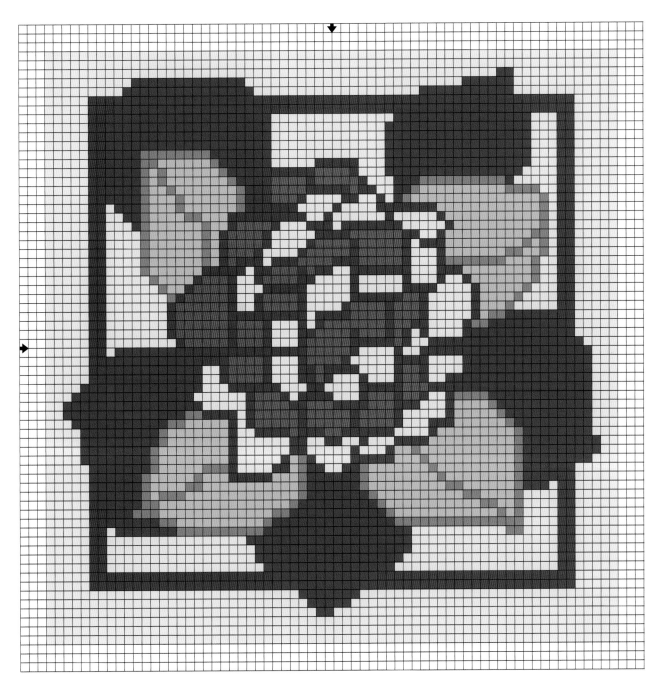

Cabbage Rose Pillow

Paisley Trivet

CATHREN BRITT

*R*ibbon, beads and snazzy fibers add a touch of whimsy to this fun paisley design. Use it in the kitchen as a trivet, or place it on an end table as an extra-large coaster. This project adds a burst of color to any decor. Enlarge the pattern, or repeat it several times on a large piece of canvas to create a great piece of wall art. This versatile project is perfect for your own home and also makes a wonderful gift.

materials

Size 5 rug canvas

25 yd. (23m) bright green fabric strips,
cut to ½" (13mm) for batik fabrics
or ¾" (2cm) for printed fabrics

8 yd. (7.5m) blue fabric strips,
cut to ½" (13mm) for batik fabrics
or ¾" (2cm) for printed fabrics

6 yd. (5.5m) teal fabric strips,
cut to ½" (13mm) for batik fabrics
or ¾" (2cm) for printed fabrics

2 yd. (2m) yellow fabric strips,
cut to ½" (13mm) for batik fabrics
or ¾" (2cm) for printed fabrics

6 yd. (5.5m) variegated blue/teal silk
ribbon, 1" (3cm) wide

6 yd. (5.5m) assorted novelty yarns

Locking medium

Locker hook

Tapestry needle

Scissors

Permanent markers

Needle and thread

25 size 8 clear seed beads

7" × 7" (18cm × 18cm) piece
of self-adhesive fabric

1 Prepare base
Cut a piece of rug canvas that measures 45 squares wide and 45 squares tall (see *Preparing the Base*, page 19). Fold under 3 squares of canvas on each edge (see *Securing the Edges of the Base*, pages 20–21). Mark the pattern from page 74 on the canvas.

2 Frame canvas
Frame the canvas with bright green fabric strips (see *Framing the Canvas*, page 21).

3 Locker hook pattern
Begin locker hooking, following the chart on page 74 or the pattern you've marked on the canvas (see *Basic Locker Hooking*, page 22). Start with the paisley motifs and work using the free-form method of locker hooking (see *Free-Form Locker Hooking*, page 25). Hold novelty yarn together with the fabric strip for the center of each motif (see *Locker Hooking with Multiple Elements*, page 26). Fill in the background of the piece with bright green fabric strips; work using the free-form method of locker hooking.

4 Embellish trivet
Using the needle and thread, sew seed beads to the paisley motifs. Sew in the yarn and fabric tail ends and the locking medium ends (see *Finishing Techniques*, pages 30–31). Cut the remaining fabric strips and ribbon into 2½" (6cm) pieces. Thread the pieces of fabric and ribbon through the edges of the trivet with the locker hook to form fringe. Tie the pieces to secure them to the trivet; trim the fabric and ribbon pieces to the same length. Line the back of the trivet with self-adhesive fabric (see *Attaching Self-Adhesive Fabric Lining*, page 32).

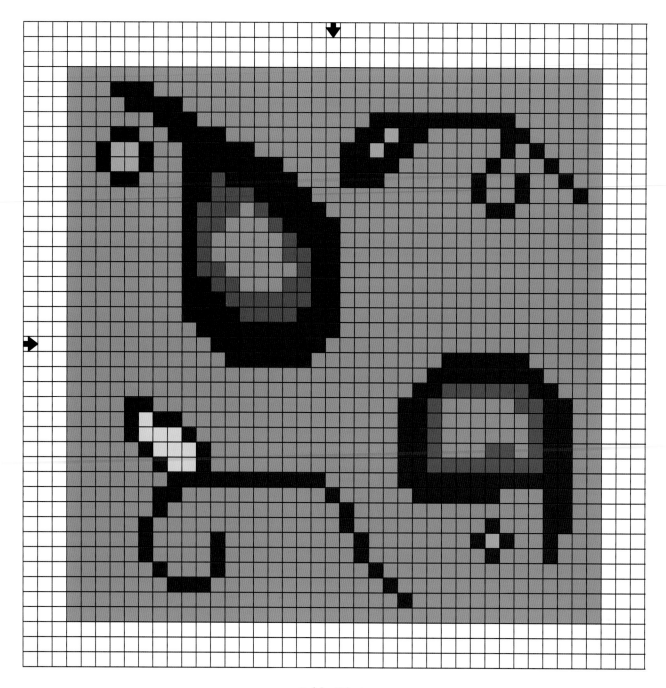

Paisley Trivet

Home Blessing Wall Hanging

CATHREN BRITT

With its folk art appeal, this fun project makes a wonderful, personalized housewarming gift. A sketch is included as a guide for this project, but for a truly personal gift, adjust the shape and colors of the project to reflect the home you want to bless. Once the locker hooking is done, add charms, beads, fibers and ribbons to decorate the home. Choose charms that have special messages for the recipient of this thoughtful, heartwarming gift.

materials

Size 5 rug canvas

20 yd. (18.5m) blue fabric strips, cut to ½" (13mm) for batik fabrics or ¾" (2cm) for printed fabrics

5 yd. (5m) brown fabric strips, cut to ½" (13mm) for batik fabrics or ¾" (2cm) for printed fabrics

5 yd. (5m) teal fabric strips, cut to ½" (13mm) for batik fabrics or ¾" (2cm) for printed fabrics

5 yd. (5m) red fabric strips, cut to ½" (13mm) for batik fabrics or ¾" (2cm) for printed fabrics

5 yd. (5m) bright green fabric strips, cut to ½" (13mm) for batik fabrics or ¾" (2cm) for printed fabrics

5 yd. (5m) yellow fabric strips, cut to ½" (13mm) for batik fabrics or ¾" (2cm) for printed fabrics

4 yd. (4m) black-and-white plaid ribbon, 1½" (4cm) wide

5 yd. (5m) assorted novelty yarns

Locking medium

Locker hook

Tapestry needle

Scissors

Permanent markers

Needle and thread

1 yd. (1m) black-and-white plaid ribbon, ⅛" (3mm) wide

Assorted buttons, beads, charms and other embellishments

7" × 10½" (18cm × 27cm) piece of self-adhesive fabric

1 Prepare base
Draw the basic outline of the home you are blessing on the rug canvas. Cut the rug canvas around the outline, leaving 2 extra squares of canvas on each side of the outline (see *Preparing the Base*, page 19). The canvas used for the project shown on page 75 measures 40 squares wide and 59 squares tall, with the top third cut into a triangle for the roof. Fold under 2 squares of canvas on each edge (see *Securing the Edges of the Base*, pages 20–21). Mark the canvas to reflect the home you are blessing, or use the sketch on page 77 for inspiration. Mark doors, windows and other features on the canvas.

2 Frame canvas
Frame the canvas with the plaid ribbon (see *Framing the Canvas*, page 21).

3 Locker hook pattern
Begin locker hooking, following the pattern you've marked on the canvas (see *Basic Locker Hooking*, page 22). Start out with the decorative elements of the pattern, such as doors and windows, and work using the free-form method of locker hooking (see *Free-Form Locker Hooking*, page 25). If desired, hold novelty yarn together with the fabric strips for any elements you wish to highlight (see *Locker Hooking with Multiple Elements*, page 26). Fill in the background of the piece with the house's colors; work using the free-form m≠≠ethod of locker hooking.

4 Embellish the house
Sew in the yarn and fabric tail ends and the locking medium ends (see *Finishing Techniques*, pages 30–31). To decorate the house, attach beads, charms, ribbons and more with ribbon or needle and thread. The piece on page 75 was embellished with charms with hopeful messages like "love," "laughter" and "peace," as well as symbolic charms including bees and dragonflies. Use embellishments that will be meaningful to the person and home you are blessing. Once you are finished embellishing, line the back of the project with self-adhesive fabric (see *Attaching Self-Adhesive Fabric Lining*, page 32).

Home Blessing Wall Hanging

gifts and accessories

There's nothing like giving a handmade gift of your own design. I love making special gifts for friends and family, so creating locker hooked gifts and accessories is what really got me "hooked" on locker hooking! This chapter features a wide variety of projects that make wonderful gifts. If you need a gift on short notice, a small project like the *Banded Bangles* on page 86 will come to your rescue. When you have a little more time, something more substantial like the *Chartreuse Blossom Bag* on page 113 will be a total showstopper. You can get creative on small projects without a big time investment: Go crazy with color choices, try unusual fibers, or add beads, ribbons, buttons or other accents for the perfect finishing touch. Each of these projects can be customized to be the perfect gift for anyone you have in mind. And not just gifts are included in this chapter: There's also a project you can make to hold a gift! Try the *Flowering Gift Bag* on page 88 to present a gift in a special way.

Don't stop at making gifts for others, either! Be sure to make a few great pieces for yourself, too. Try the *Floral Splash Panel* on page 121 to spruce up a casual bag for a day of shopping or the *Blueberry Mocha Clutch* on page 93 for an evening out. The *Shimmering Journal Cover* on page 104 can help house your thoughts while the *TechnoCozies* on page 99 can house your music, your camera or your cell phone. I urge you to try different things. There is so much more to explore and create with locker hooking!

Tic-Tac-Toe Game Board

THERESA PULIDO

This little game board makes a great gift; in addition to being fun to play with, it also looks cool displayed on an end table. Try expanding the pattern to create a game board for checkers or chess. Continue the creativity for this project with the game pieces. It's easy to make your own with polymer clay, or go hunting for fun and unique game pieces at craft stores, thrift shops or even look for hidden treasures around the house.

materials

Size 5 rug canvas

22 yd. (20.5m) blue fabric strips,
cut to ½" (13mm) for batik fabrics
or ¾" (2cm) for printed fabrics

22 yd. (20.5m) bright green fabric strips,
cut to ½" (13mm) for batik fabrics
or ¾" (2cm) for printed fabrics

13 yd. (12m) black fabric strips,
cut to ½" (13mm) for batik fabrics
or ¾" (2cm) for printed fabrics

7 yd. (6.5m) black-and-white checkered ribbon, ½" (13mm) wide

Locking medium

Locker hook

Tapestry needle

Scissors

Permanent markers

Game pieces

1 Prepare base
Cut a piece of rug canvas that measures 51 squares wide and 51 squares tall (see *Preparing the Base*, page 19). Fold under 3 squares of canvas on each edge (see *Securing the Edges of the Base*, pages 20–21). Mark the pattern from page 82 on the canvas.

2 Frame canvas
Frame the canvas with the black-and-white checkered ribbon (see *Framing the Canvas*, page 21).

3 Locker hook pattern
Begin locker hooking, following the chart on page 82 or the pattern you've marked on the canvas (see *Basic Locker Hooking*, page 22). Start with the border and work using the spiral method of locker hooking (see *Spiral Locker Hooking*, page 24). Next, work the center using the linear method of locker hooking (see *Linear Locker Hooking*, page 24).

4 Finish game board
Once the locker hooking is complete, sew in the fabric tail ends and the locking medium ends (see *Finishing Techniques*, pages 30–31). If desired, create game pieces (see page 82 for instructions).

Creating Game Pieces

1 **Begin game piece**
Condition the polymer clay and roll it out to a ⅜"
(1cm) thickness. Cut the clay into an X or O.

2 **Finish game piece**
Repeat Step 1 to create 5 X game pieces and 5 O
game pieces. Round the edges of the clay pieces and
bake following the manufacturer's instructions. If
desired, paint or embellish the game pieces.

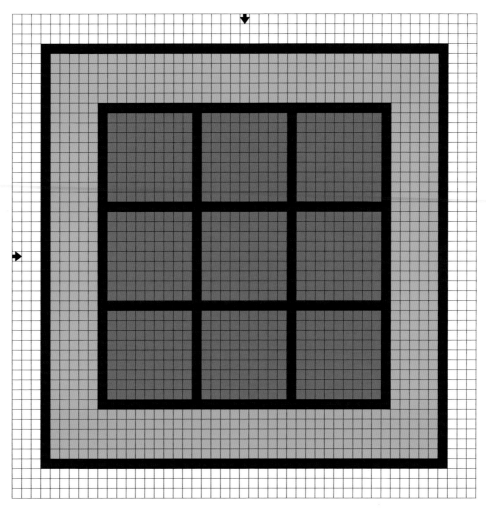

Tic-Tac-Toe Game Board

Starry Night Ornaments

CINDY SADOWSKI

Decorate your tree with these enchanting locker hooked stars for a charming display of color and creativity. You can easily locker hook a set of stars in your favorite colors or try this project as a way to use leftover fabrics in a creative way. These cheerful stars also make a great holiday gift. Or, add a special touch to a wrapped gift by attaching one of these stars instead of a bow. It's sure to be something the recipient will treasure.

materials

Size 3.75 rug canvas

7 yd. (6.5m) fabric strips for the center of the star, cut to ¾" (2cm) for batik fabrics or 1" (3cm) for printed fabrics

6 yd. (5.5m) fabric strips for the border of the star, cut to ¾" (2cm) for batik fabrics or 1" (3cm) for printed fabrics

2 yd. (2m) fabric strips for framing the star, cut to ¾" (2cm) for batik fabrics or 1" (3cm) for printed fabrics

Locking medium

Locker hook

Tapestry needle

Scissors

Permanent markers

7" × 7" (18cm × 18cm) piece of self-adhesive fabric

1 Prepare base
Draw the outline of the star pattern found on page 85 on the rug canvas. Cut the rug canvas on the marked lines (see *Preparing the Base*, page 19). Do not leave any excess canvas around the outline. Mark the pattern from page 85 on the canvas.

2 Frame canvas
Frame the canvas with fabric strips (see *Framing the Canvas*, page 21). You may need to double loop the edges in each square for full coverage.

3 Locker hook pattern
Begin locker hooking, following the chart on page 85 or the pattern you've marked on the canvas (see *Basic Locker Hooking*, page 22). Start with the border and work toward the center using the spiral method of locker hooking (see *Spiral Locker Hooking*, page 24). After the border is complete, continue working toward the center of the star in the spiral method with the fabric strips you chose for the center.

4 Finish ornament
Once the locker hooking is complete, sew in the fabric tail ends and the locking medium ends (see *Finishing Techniques*, pages 30–31). Line the back of the project with self-adhesive fabric (see *Attaching Self-Adhesive Fabric Lining*, page 32).

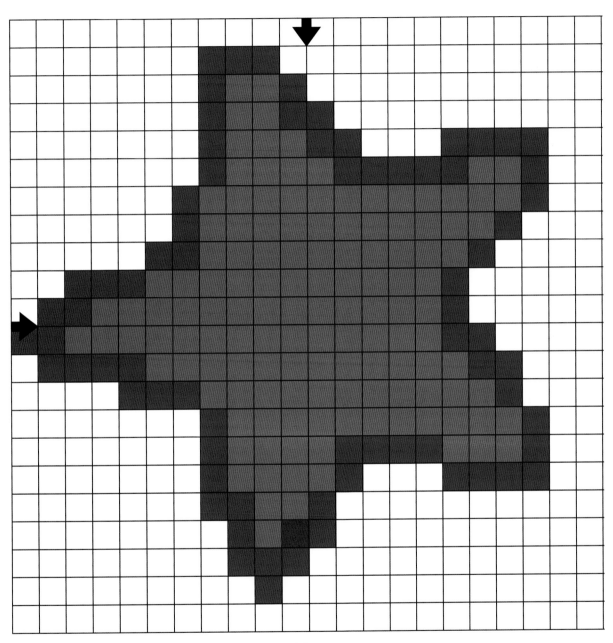

Starry Night Ornament

Banded Bangles

These fashionable bracelets are as easy to make as they are fun to wear. They look wonderful in traditional locker hooking materials, but since you need so little fabric to finish one, why not treat yourself to a luxurious fabric or ribbon when you make your bangle? I found some strips of recycled sari fabric that unraveled beautifully, creating a fuzzy fringed look. The colors are so rich and vibrant; they create an exotic tapestry with little spots of metallic interspersed. A sheer ribbon creates a completely different look with a subtle shimmer over the fabric strips. To take it further, add seed beads or other embellishments for extra sparkle.

materials

Size 5 rug canvas

25 yd. (23m) fabric strips, cut to ½" (13mm) for batik fabrics or ¾" (2cm) for printed fabrics

25 yd. (23m) ribbon or yarn to carry along with fabric (optional)

Locking medium

Locker hook

Tapestry needle

Scissors

Embellishments (optional)

1 Prepare base
Cut a piece of rug canvas for your bracelet (see *Preparing the Base*, page 19). For a small bracelet, cut the canvas to 49 squares wide and 14 squares tall; for a medium bracelet cut it 54 squares wide and 14 squares tall; for a large bracelet cut it 56 squares wide and 14 squares tall. Fold under 2 squares of canvas on each long edge (see *Securing the Edges of the Base*, pages 20–21).

2 Frame canvas
Frame both long edges of the strip of canvas, joining the canvas to form a circle as you frame by overlapping 4 squares of canvas (see *Framing the Canvas*, page 21, and *Working in the Round*, page 29).

3 Locker hook pattern
Begin locker hooking (see *Basic Locker Hooking*, page 22). Start with the bottom row and work using the linear method of locker hooking (see *Linear Locker Hooking*, page 24). Change colors or fabrics as desired.

4 Finish bracelet
Once the locker hooking is complete, sew in the fabric tail ends and the locking medium ends (see *Finishing Techniques*, pages 30–31). Embellish as desired.

Flowering Gift Bag

THERESA PULIDO

This simple burlap gift bag is easy to make and is a special way to package a small gift. The burlap adds an organic, natural feel that makes for a charming gift. The pattern shown here is very simple and is a lovely accent for this bag, but you can also create more elaborate designs. Burlap is perfect for free-form locker hooking designs, so feel free to get creative!

materials

Undyed burlap

6 yd. (5.5m) green wool fabric strips, cut to ¼" (6mm)

3 yd. (3m) gold silk fabric strips, cut to ½" (13mm)

3 yd. (3m) yellow fabric strips, cut to ½" (13mm) for batik fabrics or ¾" (2cm) for printed fabrics

Locking medium

Locker hook

Tapestry needle

Scissors

Permanent markers

Fabric glue

Iron

2 4" × 5" (10cm × 13cm) pieces of self-adhesive fabric

24" (61cm) ¾"-wide (2cm) ribbon

1 Prepare pieces
Cut 2 6" × 7" (15cm × 18cm) pieces of burlap and 1 18" × 4½" (46cm × 11cm) piece of burlap (see *Preparing the Base*, page 19). Fold over ½" (13mm) of burlap on each edge of each piece of burlap and press with an iron (see *Securing the Edges of the Base*, pages 20–21). Mark the pattern below on 1 or both 6" × 7" (15cm × 18cm) pieces of burlap.

2 Locker hook pattern
Begin locker hooking, following the sketch below or the pattern you've marked on the burlap (see *Basic Locker Hooking*, page 22). Work using the free-form method of locker hooking (see *Free-Form Locker Hooking*, page 25). Locker hook on both 6" × 7" (15cm × 18cm) pieces of burlap.

3 Assemble bag
Once the locker hooking is complete, sew in the fabric tail ends and the locking medium ends (see *Finishing Techniques*, pages 30–31). Line the back of the locker hooked pieces of burlap with self-adhesive fabric (see *Attaching Self-Adhesive Fabric Lining*, page 32). Apply glue to the folded-under seam allowance of the 18" × 4½" (46cm × 11cm) piece of burlap and adhere it to a locker hooked piece of burlap. Allow the glue to dry, then attach the other locker hooked piece. Once all the fabric glue has dried, topstitch the edges with the remaining green wool fabric strips. Cut the ribbon in half. Thread the tapestry needle with a piece of ribbon and thread each end of the ribbon through the top of the bag's edge. Tie the ends of the ribbon in knots to secure it to the bag. Seal the knots with a drop of fabric glue. Repeat on the other side for the second handle.

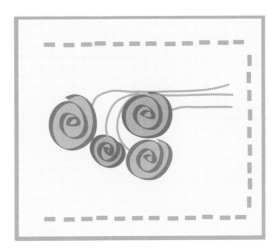

Market Basket

THERESA PULIDO

T his lovely basket is another great project that takes locker hooking into three dimensions. Two pieces of canvas are locker hooked, then a quick assembly transforms them into a useful and beautiful basket for your kitchen, dining room or office. When it is harvest time in my garden, I can't have enough baskets! You'll find them everywhere in my house, overflowing with ripe vegetables, fruit and flowers. In between harvests, baskets are useful in so many other ways. This basket is easy to modify to suit your needs. Whether you need a bread basket for your dining room table or a creative inbox for your office, this basket is up to the task.

materials

Size 5 rug canvas

105 yd. (96m) copper fabric strips, cut to ½" (13mm) for batik fabrics or ¾" (2cm) for printed fabrics

35 yd. (32m) blue fabric strips, cut to ½" (13mm) for batik fabrics or ¾" (2cm) for printed fabrics

15 yd. (14m) sheer copper ribbon, ¾" (2cm) thick

Locking medium

Locker hook

Tapestry needle

Scissors

Permanent markers

1 Prepare canvas
Cut a piece of rug canvas for the bottom of the basket that measures 43 squares wide and 43 squares tall (see *Preparing the Base*, page 19). Fold under 3 squares of canvas on each edge (see *Securing the Edges of the Base*, pages 20–21). Cut a piece of rug canvas for the sides of the basket that measures 156 squares wide and 31 squares tall. Fold under 3 squares of canvas on the top and bottom edge of this piece of canvas. Do not fold the short sides of this piece of canvas under. Mark the pattern from page 92 on the canvas.

2 Frame canvas
Frame the top edge only on the piece of rug canvas that will make up the sides of the basket (see *Framing the Canvas*, page 21). As you frame the top edge, join the piece of canvas to work in the round, overlapping the edges of the canvas for a width of 4 squares (see *Working in the Round*, page 29). Do not frame any other edge of the piece of canvas that will make up the basket's sides, and do not frame the piece of canvas that will make up the basket's bottom. These edges need to be left exposed for assembly.

3 Locker hook pattern
Begin locker hooking the basket's sides, following the chart on page 92 or the pattern you've marked on the canvas (see *Basic Locker Hooking*, page 22). Start with the top edge and work using the linear method of locker hooking (see *Linear Locker Hooking*, page 24). For the first 3 rows, hold the ribbon on top of the fabric strips and hook extra long loops (about ½" [13mm] high) to create a raised border (see *Locker Hooking with Multiple Elements*, page 26). Next, locker hook the bottom of the basket using only copper fabric strips; work using the linear method of locker hooking.

4 Finish basket
Once the locker hooking is complete, sew in the fabric tail ends and the locking medium ends (see *Finishing Techniques*, pages 30–31). Sew the basket sides to the basket bottom (see *Assembling a Project*, page 33).

Market Basket

Blueberry Mocha Clutch

THERESA PULIDO

The idea of an elegant locker hooked design may seem at odds with the nature of the materials, but this is just not so. Mohair gives this clutch a wonderful, soft feel. The luxurious look and feel of silk also add elegance to this project. This stylish and versatile handbag is great for casual events and for evening outings, too. It's perfect with a great pair of denim jeans but works just as well with stylish evening attire. Try new color combinations so it matches your outfit perfectly!

materials

Size 5 rug canvas

60 yd. (55m) brown fabric strips, cut to ½" (13mm) for batik fabrics or ¾" (2cm) for printed fabrics

24 yd. (22m) blue silk fabric strips, cut to ½" (13mm)

10 yd. (9.5m) light blue silk fabric strips, cut to ½" (13mm)

55 yd. (50.5m) brown mohair yarn

Locking medium

Locker hook

Tapestry needle

Scissors

Permanent markers

Fabric glue

Needle and thread

Iron

10¾" × 10¾" (27cm × 27cm) piece of silk cloth that coordinates with the fabric strips

9½" × 6½" (24cm × 17cm) piece of stabilizer or heavy fusible web

Magnetic snap

1 Prepare base

Cut a piece of rug canvas that measures 58 squares wide and 62 squares tall (see *Preparing the Base*, page 19). Cut 2 pieces of rug canvas that measure 10 squares wide and 22 squares tall. Fold under 3 squares of canvas on each edge of each piece of canvas (see *Securing the Edges of the Base*, pages 20–21). Mark the pattern from page 95 on the canvas.

2 Locker hook pattern

Begin locker hooking on the larger piece of canvas, following the chart on page 95 or the pattern you've marked on the canvas (see *Basic Locker Hooking*, page 22). Start with the floral element and work using the free-form method of locker hooking (see *Free-Form Locker Hooking*, page 25). Locker hook the rest of the design using the linear method of locker hooking (see *Linear Locker Hooking*, page 24). In all areas that are locker hooked with the brown fabric, carry the mohair yarn along with the fabric strips (see *Locker Hooking with Multiple Elements*, page 26). Next, locker hook the smaller pieces of canvas using the linear method.

3 Assemble bag

Once the locker hooking is complete, sew in the fabric tail ends and the locking medium ends (see *Finishing Techniques*, pages 30–31). Sew the locker hooked pieces of canvas together to form a pouch (see *Assembling a Project*, page 33). Frame the edges of the flap and the edges around the bag's opening (see *Framing the Canvas*, page 21).

4 Line bag

Fold over a ½" (13mm) seam allowance on each side of the coordinating fabric and steam press it down. Measure the fabric against the locker hooked piece and adjust the fabric to match; steam press any adjustments. Follow the manufacturer's instructions to attach half of the magnetic snap at the center top edge of the lining fabric. Attach stabilizer or heavy fusible web to the bottom portion of the lining following the manufacturer's instructions. Slip the lining fabric into the pouch. Using fabric glue, adhere the back of the magnetic snap on the lining to the locker hooked canvas. Allow the glue to dry completely. Gluing the snap to the fabric makes the snap more secure. Slip stitch the lining to the top flap of the pouch (see *Sewing on Fabric*, page 32). Fold the flap over the pouch and mark the spot where the magnetic snap meets the other piece of locker hooked canvas. Attach the second half of the magnetic snap at the mark on the clutch. Finish slip stitching the lining into the pouch.

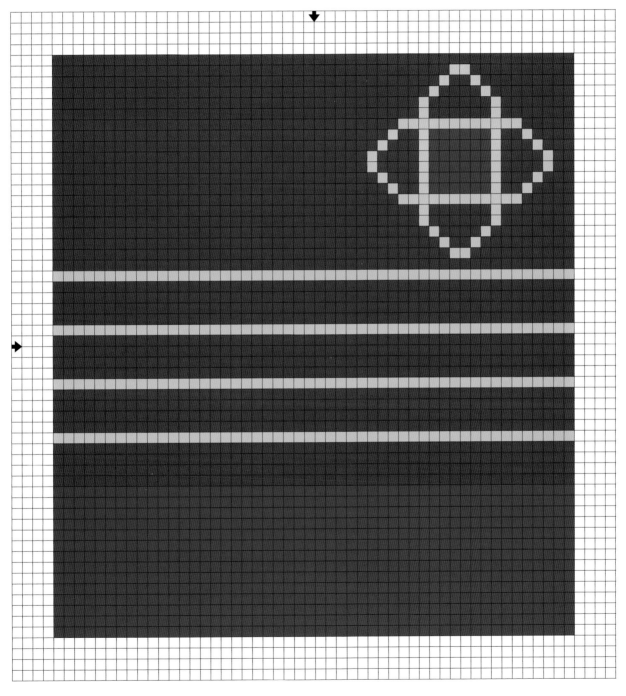

Blueberry Mocha Clutch

Victorian Sachets

THERESA PULIDO

These elegant Victorian sachets make excellent gifts. Try filling them with lavender, rose petals or your favorite sachet blend. They're a nearly no-sew project you can make quickly and easily with a simple stitch across the top closure to seal in the sachet filler. Experiment with different floral designs and color combinations. Try using different ribbons and beads for embellishing.

materials

ROSE SACHET

Undyed burlap

6 yd. (5.5m) pink silk fabric strips, cut to ½" (13mm)

3 yd. (3m) sheer pink ribbon, ⅝" (16mm) wide

½ yd. (0.5m) pink ribbon, ¼" (6mm) wide

Locking medium

Locker hook

Tapestry needle

Scissors

Permanent markers

Fabric glue

Iron

2 pink crystal beads

Dried rose petals or sachet blend

Rose Sachet

1 Prepare pieces
Cut a 14" × 5" (36cm × 13cm) piece of burlap (see *Preparing the Base*, page 19). Fold over ½" (13mm) on each edge of the burlap and press with an iron (see *Securing the Edges of the Base*, pages 20–21). Mark the pattern below on the burlap.

2 Locker hook pattern
Begin locker hooking, following the sketch below or the pattern you've marked on the burlap (see *Basic Locker Hooking*, page 22). Work using the free-form method of locker hooking (see *Free-Form Locker Hooking*, page 25).

3 Assemble sachet
Once the locker hooking is complete, sew in the fabric tail ends and the locking medium ends (see *Finishing Techniques*, pages 30–31). Apply glue to the folded-under seam allowance of the burlap, fold the piece in half and adhere to form a pouch. Allow the glue to dry completely. Once all of the fabric glue has dried, fill the pouch with dried rose petals or your favorite sachet blend. Sew the opening at the top closed with the 2 ribbons held together. Tie the ribbons together at the side of the pouch. Embellish the ribbons with beads.

Undyed burlap

**4 yd. (4m) green wool fabric strips,
cut to ¼" (6mm)**

**2 yd. (2m) purple wool fabric strips,
cut to ¼" (6mm)**

**1 yd. (1m) purple fabric strips,
cut to ½" (13mm) for batik fabrics
or ¾" (2cm) for printed fabrics**

1 yd. (1m) purple bulky wool yarn

**2 yd. (2m) variegated blue/green/purple
ribbon, ¼" (6mm) wide**

Locking medium

Locker hook

Tapestry needle

Scissors

Permanent markers

Fabric glue

Iron

1 blue crystal bead

1 purple crystal bead

Dried lavender

Lavender Sachet

1 Prepare pieces
Cut a 14" × 5" (36cm × 13cm) piece of burlap (see *Preparing the Base*, page 19). Fold over ½" (13mm) on each edge of the burlap and press with an iron (see *Securing the Edges of the Base*, pages 20–21). Mark the pattern below on the burlap.

2 Locker hook pattern
Begin locker hooking, following the sketch below or the pattern you've marked on the burlap (see *Basic Locker Hooking*, page 22). Work using the free-form method of locker hooking (see *Free-Form Locker Hooking*, page 25).

3 Assemble sachet
Once the locker hooking is complete, sew in the fabric tail ends and the locking medium ends (see *Finishing Techniques*, pages 30–31). Apply glue to the folded-under seam allowance of the burlap, fold the piece in half and adhere to form a pouch. Allow the glue to dry completely. Once all of the fabric glue has dried, fill the pouch with dried lavender. Sew the opening at the top closed with the ribbon. Tie the ribbon at the side of the pouch. Embellish the ribbon with beads.

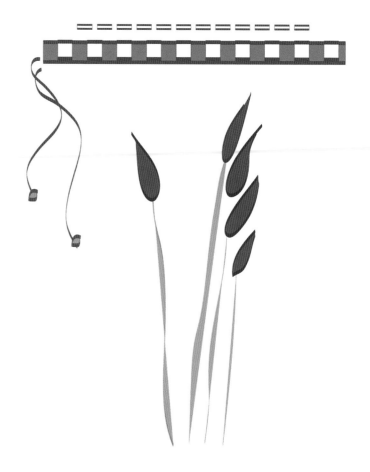

TechnoCozies

THERESA PULIDO

*T*he great thing about this small project is that you can finish the locker hooking quickly and then you can have fun embellishing with beads, buttons and more. You can also get really creative with the locker hooking materials and make it whatever you want, from elegant to wild. Want to stash your technological toys in a swanky way? Try silk for locker hooking. In the mood for something more playful? How about some bright rainbow strips? These three designs show a few of your options. Small and cozy to hold, but large enough for your cell phone, camera or MP3 player, plus ID, credit cards and lip gloss—what else could you need?

materials

Size 5 rug canvas

38 yd. (35m) cotton, wool or silk fabric strips, cut to ½" (13mm) for batik fabrics or ¾" (2cm) for printed fabrics

Up to 38 yd. (35m) ribbon or yarn to carry along with fabric (optional)

Locking medium

Locker hook

Tapestry needle

Scissors

Permanent markers

Fabric glue

Needle and thread

6" (15cm) piece of thin ribbon or yarn

Beads

Buttons

Additional embellishments

1 Prepare base

Cut a piece of rug canvas that measures 18 squares wide and 54 squares tall (see *Preparing the Base*, page 19). Cut 2 pieces of rug canvas that measure 9 squares wide and 19 squares tall. Fold under 2 squares of canvas on each edge of each piece of canvas and glue down the folded canvas (see *Securing the Edges of the Base*, pages 20–21). Mark the pattern from page 101 on the canvas.

2 Locker hook pattern

Begin locker hooking on the larger piece of canvas, following a chart on page 101 or the pattern you've marked on the canvas (see *Basic Locker Hooking*, page 22). Start in the top right corner and locker hook the design using the linear method of locker hooking (see *Linear Locker Hooking*, page 24). You can work either vertically or horizontally. If desired, carry yarn or ribbon along with the fabric strips (see *Locker Hooking with Multiple Elements*, page 26). Next, locker hook the 2 smaller pieces of canvas using the linear method of locker hooking. Work either vertically or horizontally to match the larger piece of canvas.

3 Assemble cozy

Once the locker hooking is complete, sew in the fabric ends and the locking medium ends (see *Finishing Techniques*, pages 30–31). Sew the locker hooked pieces of canvas together to form a pouch (see *Assembling a Project*, page 33). Frame the unfinished edges of the pouch (see *Framing the Canvas*, page 21). Sew a large bead or button to the front of the bottom flap of the pouch. Thread a piece of ribbon or yarn through the top flap of the pouch; knot the first end to secure the yarn to the flap. Seal the knot with a dot of glue. String 1 or more beads on the opposite end of the yarn or ribbon and tie a knot in that end. Secure the second knot with a dot of glue.

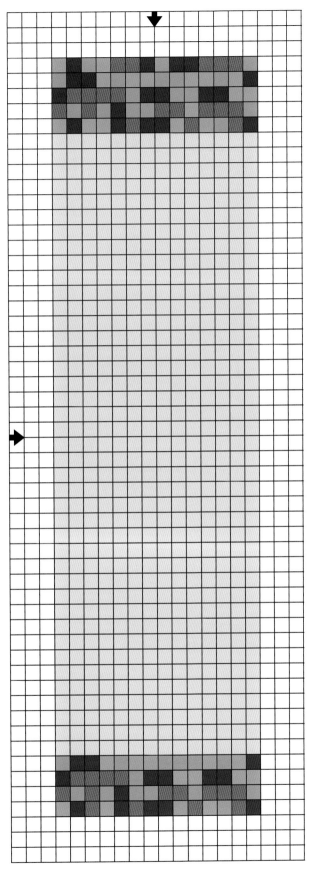

TechnoCozies

Drink Keeper

THERESA PULIDO

*L*ocker hooking is not a craft that easily lends itself to making gifts for men, but I finally found the perfect project for all the men in your life. This drink holder, or "koozy" as my husband calls it, can be customized with your favorite guy in mind. Make it in school or team colors, or add a team symbol, initial or monogram, and you have the perfect, personal gift to give your favorite guy. I branded this one with a C for my husband, Chris.

materials

Size 5 rug canvas

45 yd. (41.5m) bright green fabric strips, cut to ½" (13mm) for batik fabrics or ¾" (2cm) for printed fabrics

13 yd. (12m) dark green fabric strips, cut to ½" (13mm) for batik fabrics or ¾" (2cm) for printed fabrics

5 yd. (5m) yellow fabric strips, cut to ½" (13mm) for batik fabrics or ¾" (2cm) for printed fabrics

Locking medium

Locker hook

Tapestry needle

Scissors

Permanent markers

1 Prepare canvas
Cut a piece of rug canvas for the bottom of the drink holder that measures 15 squares wide and 15 squares tall (see *Preparing the Base*, page 19). Fold under 2 squares of canvas on each edge (see *Securing the Edges of the Base*, pages 20–21). Cut a piece of rug canvas for the sides of the drink holder that measures 53 squares wide and 35 squares tall. Fold under 3 squares of canvas on the top and bottom edges of this piece of canvas. Do not fold the canvas under on the short sides of the canvas. Mark the pattern below on the canvas.

2 Frame canvas
Frame the top edge only on the piece of rug canvas that will make up the sides of the drink holder (see *Framing the Canvas*, page 21). As you frame the top edge, join the piece of canvas to work in the round, overlapping the edges of the canvas for a width of 4 squares (see *Working in the Round*, page 29). Do not frame any other edge on either of the canvas pieces. These edges need to be left exposed for assembly later.

3 Locker hook pattern
Begin locker hooking the drink holder's sides, following the chart below or the pattern you've marked on the canvas (see *Basic Locker Hooking*, page 22). Start with the top edge and work using the linear method of locker hooking (see *Linear Locker Hooking*, page 24). Next, locker hook the bottom of the drink holder; start in the center and work using the spiral method of locker hooking (see *Spiral Locker Hooking*, page 24).

4 Finish drink holder
Once the locker hooking is complete, sew in the fabric tail ends and the locking medium ends (see *Finishing Techniques*, pages 30–31). Sew the drink holder's sides to the bottom (see *Assembling a Project*, page 33).

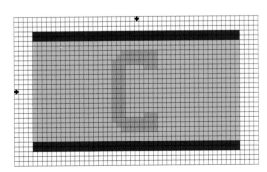

Shimmering Journal Cover

CATHREN BRITT

This beautiful journal cover incorporates some unusual fiber finds and a collection of gorgeous ribbons, too. The vintage mother of pearl button and the soft touch of glitter on the inside add a glimmering glow to the design. This journal cover is perfectly reusable and can be freshened with a new journal as needed. It makes a great gift for anyone that likes to keep a journal or has been thinking about writing. Any artist would appreciate a sketchbook wrapped in this lovely cover, as well. This type of cover can also be customized to fit a special photo album, wedding album or guest book, too.

materials

Size 5 rug canvas

A variety of ½" (13mm) wide ribbons, yarns and fabric strips totaling 75 yd. (69m)

Locking medium

Locker hook

Tapestry needle

Scissors

Permanent markers

Fabric glue

Needle and thread

Large button

Tan fabric paint

Gold glitter

5" × 8" (13cm × 20cm) blank journal

1 Prepare base
Cut a piece of rug canvas that measures 82 squares wide and 42 squares tall (see *Preparing the Base*, page 19). Mark the pattern from page 106 on the canvas, centering the pattern. Portions on the left and right sides of the canvas will be unmarked. Paint the unmarked portions of canvas with tan fabric paint. Allow the paint to dry completely. Brush the painted portions of the canvas with fabric glue and lightly sprinkle gold glitter on the canvas. Allow the glue to dry completely.

2 Frame canvas
Frame the canvas with your choice of fabric strips or ribbon (see *Framing the Canvas*, page 21).

3 Locker hook pattern
Begin locker hooking, following the chart on page 106 or the pattern you've marked on the canvas (see *Basic Locker Hooking*, page 22). Start at the top row and work using the spiral method of locker hooking (see *Spiral Locker Hooking*, page 24). Leave 15 rows of canvas unhooked on each short side of the canvas.

4 Finish journal cover
Once the locker hooking is complete, sew in the fabric tail ends and the locking medium ends (see *Finishing Techniques*, pages 30–31). Fold over the canvas on each side where the locker hooked portion ends. Whip stitch the unhooked canvas edges to the hooked canvas. Frame the folded edges. Sew a button to the front of the cover and a ribbon to the back of the cover to form the journal's closure.

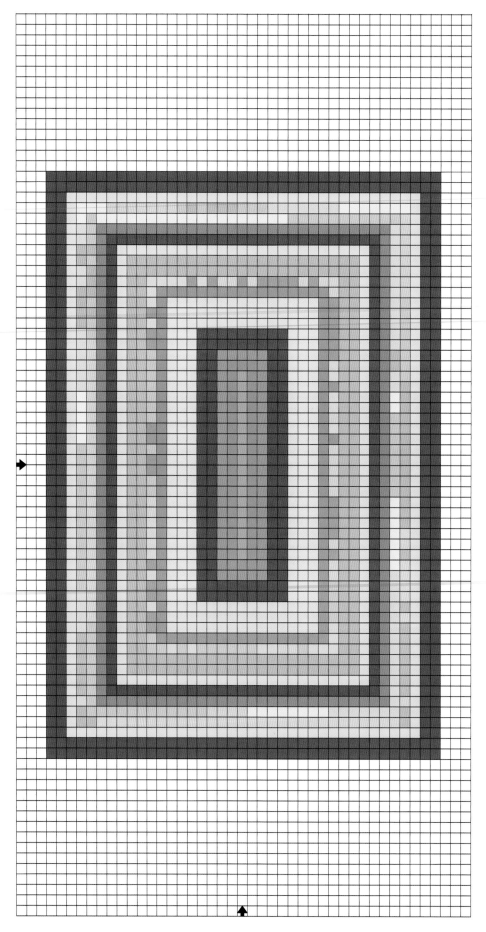

Shimmering Journal Cover

Blooming Burlap Bag

A tall burlap bag is a charming way to present a difficult-to-wrap gift. The next time you want to bring a bottle of wine or champagne to a dinner party, or even if you want to give a friend a bottle of fancy bubble bath, this bag will come to your rescue. The floral pattern and shimmering accents make any gift even more special.

materials

Undyed burlap

3 yd. (3m) green silk fabric strips, cut to ½" (13mm)

5 yd. (5m) red fabric strips, cut to ½" (13mm) for batik fabrics or ¾" (2cm) for printed fabrics

1 yd. (1m) sheer pink ribbon, ⅝" (16mm) wide

1 yd. (1m) sheer green ribbon, ⅝" (16mm) wide

6 yd. (5.5m) pink ribbon, ¼" (6mm) wide

Locking medium

Locker hook

Tapestry needle

Scissors

Permanent markers

Fabric glue

Iron

1 Prepare pieces
Cut 2 6" × 14" (15cm × 36cm) pieces of burlap and 1 32" × 5" (81cm × 13cm) piece of burlap (see *Preparing the Base*, page 19). Fold over ½" (13mm) of burlap on each edge of each piece of burlap and press with an iron (see *Securing the Edges of the Base*, pages 20–21). Mark the pattern on page 109 on one of the 6" × 14" (15cm × 36cm) pieces of burlap.

2 Locker hook pattern
Begin locker hooking, following the sketch on page 109 or the pattern you've marked on the burlap (see *Basic Locker Hooking*, page 22). Work using the free-form method of locker hooking (see *Free-Form Locker Hooking*, page 25).

3 Assemble bag
Once the locker hooking is complete, sew in the fabric tail ends and the locking medium ends (see *Finishing Techniques*, pages 30–31). Apply a bead of glue to the folded-under seam allowance of the 32" × 5" (81cm × 13cm) piece of burlap and adhere it to the locker hooked piece of burlap. Allow the glue to dry, then attach the unhooked piece of burlap. Once all of the fabric glue has dried, topstitch the edges with the ¼"-wide (6mm) ribbon. Topstitch the top edge of the locker hooked side with the sheer pink ribbon. Pull the ribbon through so that there is an equal amount of ribbon on each side of the front panel. Repeat on the back panel with the sheer green ribbon.

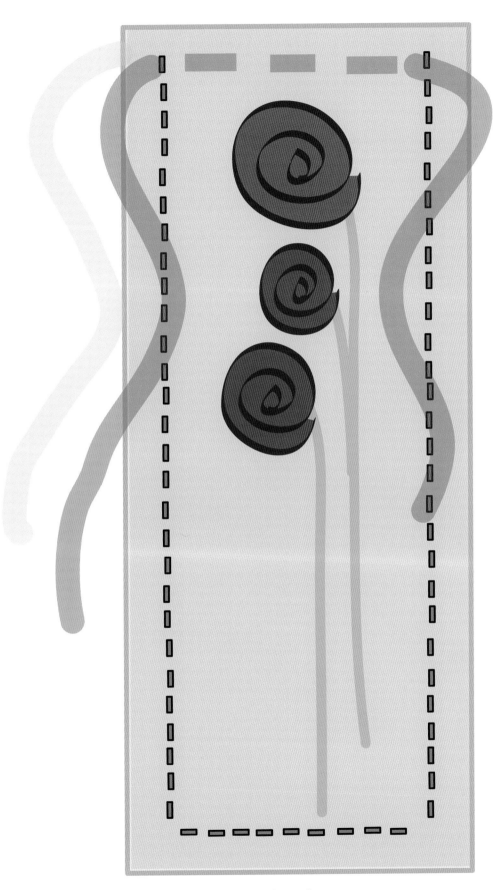

Blooming Burlap Bag

Easter Basket

THERESA PULIDO

*T*his basic basket pattern calls for a rectangular bottom and an oval body with a handle for easy carrying. I created this design with an Easter egg hunt in mind. I thought it would be the perfect place for little ones to store their treasures. This design can also be used year-round as a small tote bag or as a fun gift bearing treats inside. Adorn your baskets with a variety of fun embellishments. This one includes a simple felt flower and is accented with wildly colorful yarn.

materials

Size 5 rug canvas

52 yd. (48m) bright green fabric strips, cut to ½" (13mm) for batik fabrics or ¾" (2cm) for printed fabrics

30 yd. (27.5m) purple fabric strips, cut to ½" (13mm) for batik fabrics or ¾" (2cm) for printed fabrics

16 yd. (15m) variegated bulky novelty yarn

Locking medium

Locker hook

Tapestry needle

Scissors

Permanent markers

Fabric glue

Needle and thread

1 Prepare canvas
Cut a piece of rug canvas for the bottom of the basket that measures 21 squares wide and 36 squares tall (see *Preparing the Base*, page 19). Fold under 3 squares of canvas on each edge (see *Securing the Edges of the Base*, pages 20–21). Cut a piece of rug canvas for the handle of the basket that measures 11 squares wide and 66 squares tall. Fold under 2 squares of canvas on each edge. Cut a piece of rug canvas for the sides of the basket that measures 98 squares wide and 32 squares tall. Fold under 3 squares of canvas on the top and bottom edges of this piece of canvas. Do not fold the canvas under on the short sides of the canvas. Mark the pattern from page 112 on the canvas.

2 Frame canvas
Using fabric strips, frame the long edges only on the piece of rug canvas that will make up the handle of the basket (see *Framing the Canvas*, page 21). Frame the top edge only on the piece of rug canvas that will make up the sides of the basket. As you frame the top edge, join the piece of canvas to work in the round, overlapping the edges of the canvas for a width of 4 squares (see *Working in the Round*, page 29). Do not frame any other edge of the piece of canvas that will make up the basket's sides, and do not frame the piece of canvas that will make up the basket's bottom. These edges must be left exposed for assembly.

3 Locker hook pattern
Begin locker hooking the basket's sides, following the chart on page 112 or the pattern you've marked on the canvas (see *Basic Locker Hooking*, page 22). Start with the top edge and work using the linear method of locker hooking (see *Linear Locker Hooking*, page 24). Next, locker hook the bottom of the basket using only purple fabric strips; work using the linear method of locker hooking. Last, locker hook the basket's handle following the chart on page 112. Use the linear method of locker hooking for the handle.

4 Finish basket
Once the locker hooking is complete, sew in the fabric tail ends and the locking medium ends (see *Finishing Techniques*, pages 30–31). Sew the basket sides to the basket bottom (see *Assembling a Project*, page 33). Sew the handle to the top edges of the basket with needle and thread. Reinforce the area where the handle meets the basket with fabric glue.

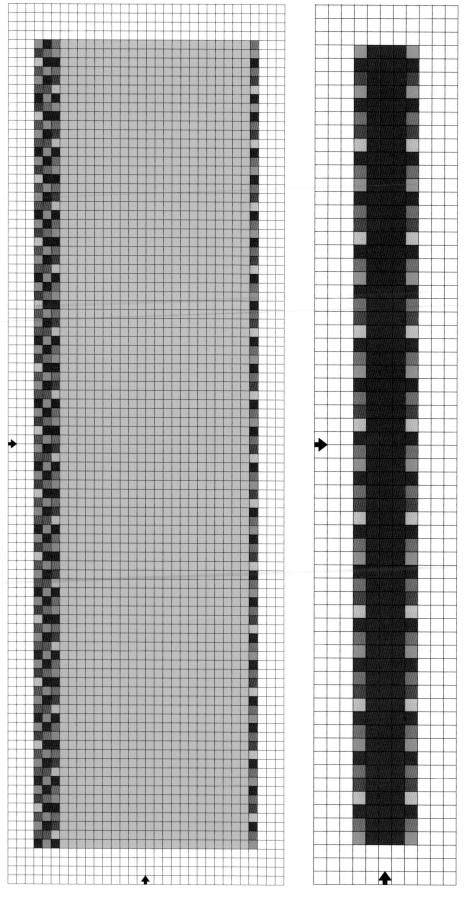

Easter Basket sides   Easter Basket handle

Chartreuse Blossom Bag

THERESA PULIDO AND SHERRI HAAB

I love the color combination of fresh green against rich brown; it's the look of plants growing in soil. So I just had to use these colors for this bag. Don't be limited by these color choices, though! This bag would look wonderful in a variety of combinations, so use your favorites. The great macramé handle adds a fun, retro touch to this bag—make it long or short to suit your needs. This version of the bag has a different design on each side. If you like one design better than the other, feel free to make both sides the same. I like using both patterns because you can flip it around and you'll have a completely different look.

materials

Size 5 rug canvas

180 yd. (165m) brown fabric strips,
cut to ½" (13mm) for batik fabrics
or ¾" (2cm) for printed fabrics

44 yd. (40.5m) bright green fabric strips,
cut to ½" (13mm) for batik fabrics or
¾" (2cm) for printed fabrics

24 yd. (22m) dark green fabric strips,
cut to ½" (13mm) for batik fabrics
or ¾" (2cm) for printed fabrics

Locking medium

Locker hook

Tapestry needle

Scissors

Permanent markers

Fabric glue

**Needle
and thread**

**6 10mm round
resin beads that
coordinate with
the fabric strips**

**7 20mm resin
disk beads that
coordinate with
the fabric strips**

1 Prepare base
Cut a piece of rug canvas that measures 21 squares wide and 130 squares tall (see *Preparing the Base*, page 19). Cut 2 pieces of rug canvas that measure 66 squares wide and 43 squares tall. Fold under 3 squares of canvas on each edge of each piece of canvas and secure by stitching the edges down (see *Securing the Edges of the Base*, pages 20–21). Mark the patterns from page 117 on the pieces of canvas.

2 Locker hook pattern
Begin locker hooking (see *Basic Locker Hooking*, page 22). Locker hook the entire 21 × 130 piece of canvas using the brown fabric strips and the linear method of locker hooking (see *Linear Locker Hooking*, page 24).

For the floral 66 × 43 piece of canvas, start by outlining each of the floral elements with brown fabric strips; work using the free-form method of locker hooking (see *Free-Form Locker Hooking*, page 25). Fill in each floral element using the free-form locker hooking method. Locker hook the background with brown fabric strips, working in the linear locker hooking method.

For the geometric 66 × 43 piece of canvas, start by working each of the squares in the spiral locker hooking method (see *Spiral Locker Hooking*, page 24). Start at the top right corner of each square and work toward the center. Locker hook the background with brown fabric strips, using the linear locker hooking method.

3 Assemble bag
Once the locker hooking is complete, sew in the fabric tail ends and the locking medium ends (see *Finishing Techniques*, pages 30–31). Sew the locker hooked pieces of canvas together (see *Assembling a Project*, page 33). Frame the opening of the bag (see *Framing the Canvas*, page 21). Macramé the purse handle (see page 115 for instructions). Attach the handle to the bag by sewing down an end of the handle on each side of the bag. Secure the handle to the bag with fabric glue.

Creating a Macramé Handle

1 Begin strap
Cut 4 5' (1.5m) strips of brown fabric. Fold the strips in half and tie an overhand knot at the folded end. Anchor the knot to something sturdy, such as a chair back or couch arm. This strap is made using square knots, which are composed of 2 half knots. Begin the first half knot by separating the 4 leftmost fabric strips. For clarity, these strips are referred to by number from left to right in the instructions. Fold strip 1 over strips 2 and 3.

2 Complete first half knot
Bring strip 4 over strip 1, and then under strips 2 and 3, coming up through the loop that strip 1 created. Strip 4 has now become strip 1, and strip 1 has become strip 4. Tighten this half knot by pulling strips 1 and 4 up toward the top of the strap.

3 Complete square knot
To complete a square knot, tie a second half knot that is the reverse of the first. Fold strip 4 over strips 2 and 3. Bring strip 1 over strip 4, and then under strips 2 and 3, coming up through the loop that strip 4 created. Tighten this knot as well.

4 Continue strap
Repeat Steps 1–3 with the 4 rightmost strips, then with the 4 center strips. Start the knotting pattern again with the 4 leftmost strips.

5 Finish strap
After repeating the knotting pattern (left, right, center) 3 times, thread a large resin bead onto the 2 center strips. Tie a square knot on either side of the bead using 3 strips instead of 4 (there will be only 1 strip in the center of the square knot instead of 2). Tie a square knot with the four center strips under the bead. Repeat the left, right, center knotting pattern once. String a small resin bead on the rightmost fabric strip. Repeat the knotting pattern again, then add another large resin bead to the 2 center strips between 2 of the 3-strip square knots. Tie a square knot with the 4 center strips under the bead. Repeat the knotting pattern once more. String a small resin bead on the leftmost fabric strip. Continue this pattern of knots interspersed with large beads in the center of the strap and small beads alternating on the left and right sides of the strap for 24" (61cm). End the strap with 3 repeats of the knotting pattern.

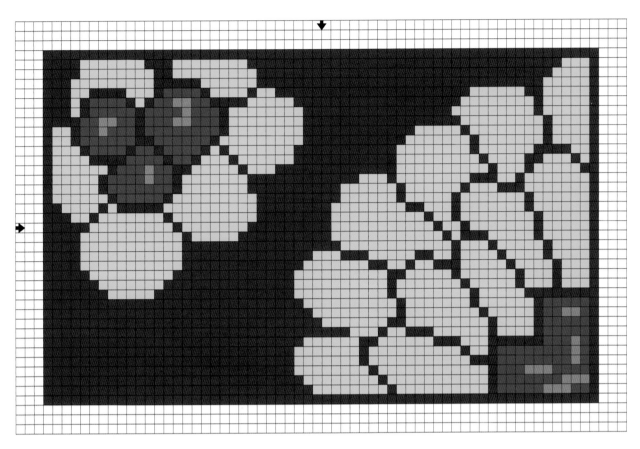

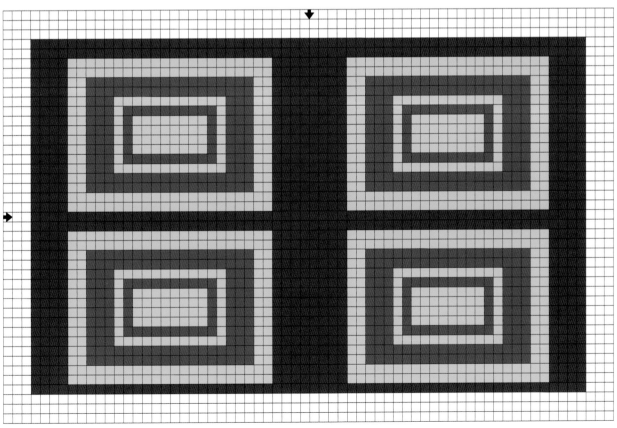

Chartreuse Blossom Bag

Two Bottle Tote

KATHLEEN CARPENTER

The colors in this tote—the red of merlot, the gold of chardonnay and the purple of ripening grapes—are perfect reflections of the wines it can carry. This tote is designed to carry two bottles of wine or other beverages and is wonderful for a picnic or as a carrier for a hostess gift. There is no need for a divider because the weight of the bottles and the shape of the carrier work to keep the bottles separated while toting them. Another unique feature of this pattern is that it combines locker hooking and crochet with a few easy steps, allowing you to try something new.

materials

Size 5 rug canvas

125 yd. (114.5m) red fabric strips, cut to ½" (13mm) for batik fabrics or ¾" (2cm) for printed fabrics

30 yd. (27.5m) purple fabric strips, cut to ½" (13mm) for batik fabrics or ¾" (2cm) for printed fabrics

44 yd. (40.5m) yellow fabric strips, cut to ½" (13mm) for batik fabrics or ¾" (2cm) for printed fabrics

Locking medium

Locker hook

Tapestry needle

Scissors

Permanent markers

US F (3.75mm) crochet hook

1 Prepare base

Cut a piece of rug canvas that measures 40 squares wide and 19 squares tall (see *Preparing the Base*, page 19). Fold under 3 squares of canvas on each edge and secure by stitching the edges down (see *Securing the Edges of the Base*, pages 20–21).Cut a piece of rug canvas that measures 98 squares wide and 48 squares tall. Fold under 3 squares of canvas on the top and bottom edges only and secure by stitching the edges down. Mark the pattern from page 120 on the 98 × 48 piece of canvas.

2 Locker hook pattern

Begin locker hooking (see *Basic Locker Hooking*, page 22). Locker hook the 40 × 19 piece of canvas using red fabric strips and the linear method of locker hooking (see *Linear Locker Hooking*, page 24).

For the 98 × 48 piece of canvas, join the canvas to work in the round, overlapping the canvas for 4 squares (see *Working in the Round*, page 29). Start locker hooking the rectangles using the spiral locker hooking method (see *Spiral Locker Hooking*, page 24). Start at the top right corner of each rectangle and work toward the center. Locker hook the red strips between the squares vertically using the linear locker hooking method. Locker hook the red strips at the top and bottom of the design horizontally using the linear method.

4 Assemble tote

Once the locker hooking is complete, sew in the fabric tail ends and the locking medium ends (see *Finishing Techniques*, pages 30–31). Sew the locker hooked pieces of canvas together (see *Assembling a Project*, page 33). Using the following pattern, crochet the handle for the carrier:

Round 1: Beginning at the side of the tote, single crochet in each square around the top of the hooked canvas edge. Slip stitch to join.

Rounds 2–4: Chain 1, single crochet in each single crochet of the previous row. Slip stitch to join.

Round 5: Chain 1, single crochet in the next 16 single crochets from the previous row, chain 12, skip 14 single crochets, single crochet in next 32 single crochets from the previous round, chain 12, skip 14 single crochets, single crochet in next 16 single crochets, slip stitch to join.

Round 6: Chain 1, single crochet in 16 single crochets, single crochet in each of the chain stitches, single crochet in 32 single crochets, single crochet in each of the chain stitches, single crochet in the next 16 single crochets, slip stitch to join.

Round 7: Chain 1, single crochet in each single crochet around. Slip stitch to join. Fasten off and sew in tails.

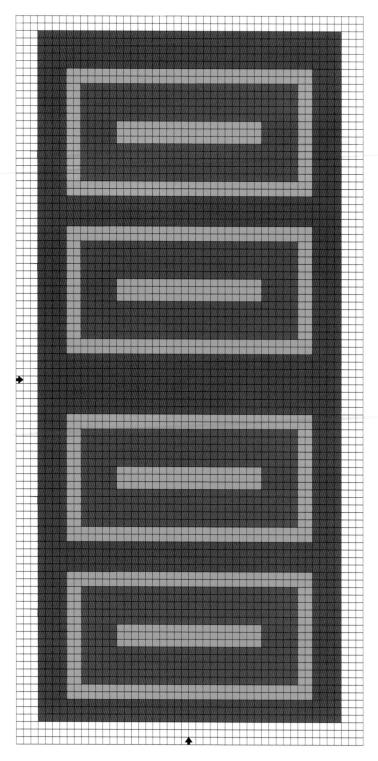

Two Bottle Tote

Floral Splash Panel

KATHLEEN CARPENTER

This design takes recycling clothing to a new level! The fabric strips used in the project were cut from a thrift store treasure: a flamboyant floral muumuu. The fabric had such a fabulous print and a great woven texture that it had to be reused for something. If you have old garments that have been sitting in the back of the closet, you can recycle them and turn them into a locker hooked design. Visiting the local vintage shop or thrift store is also a great way to find recyclable items. You can locker hook this panel and stitch it into an existing messenger bag or anything else that needs a little sprucing up. The bag shown here was made by deconstructing a pair of overalls. Visit our Web site for the pattern at www.colorcrazycrafts.com.

materials

Size 5 rug canvas

46 yd. (42m) pink fabric strips, cut to ½" (13mm) for batik fabrics or ¾" (2cm) for printed fabrics

23 yd. (21m) green fabric strips, cut to ½" (13mm) for batik fabrics or ¾" (2cm) for printed fabrics

15 yd. (14m) pink mohair yarn

2 yd. (2m) red eyelash yarn

Locking medium

Locker hook

Tapestry needle

Scissors

Permanent markers

Messenger bag

Needle and thread

1 **Prepare base**
Cut a piece of rug canvas that measures 61 squares wide and 26 squares tall (see *Preparing the Base*, page 19). Fold under 3 squares of canvas on each edge (see *Securing the Edges of the Base*, pages 20–21). Mark the pattern from page 123 on the canvas.

2 **Frame canvas**
Frame the canvas with the pink fabric strips (see *Framing the Canvas*, page 21).

3 **Locker hook pattern**
Begin locker hooking, following the chart on page 123 or the pattern you've marked on the canvas (see *Basic Locker Hooking*, page 22). Start with the center of the flower and work outward using the free-form method of locker hooking (see *Free-Form Locker Hooking*, page 25). Next, work the rest of the flower using the free-form method. Work the green stem and leaves next and, finally, fill in the background of the piece with pink fabric strips using the free-form method of locker hooking.

4 **Finish panel**
Once the locker hooking is complete, sew in the fabric tail ends and the locking medium ends (see *Finishing Techniques*, pages 30–31). Use a needle and thread to sew the panel to the messenger bag.

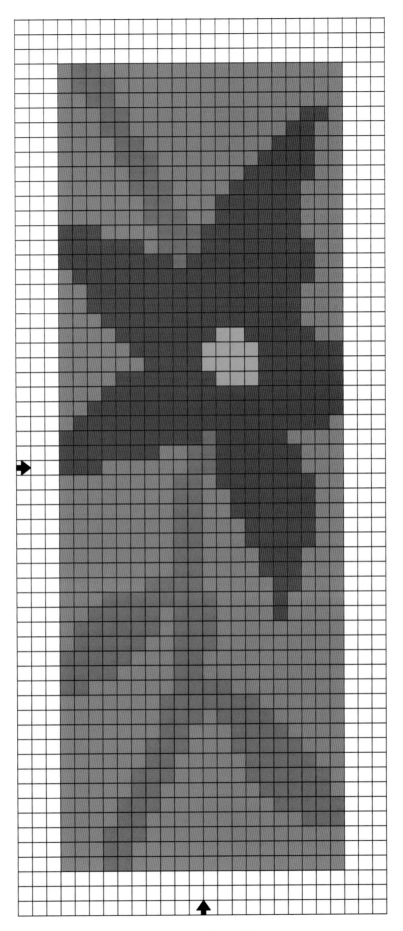

Floral Splash Panel

resources

Basic locker hooking supplies are easy to find in most craft stores, so try your local shops first. If you have trouble finding locker hooking supplies locally, or you're looking for a certain something to add to a project, try the stores and Web sites listed here. They are some of my favorite suppliers!

Basic Locker Hooking Tools & Supplies

Beacon Adhesives
www.beaconadhesives.com

Ben Franklin Crafts
www.benfranklinstores.com

Crafts, Etc!
www.craftsetc.com

Hobby Lobby
www.hobbylobby.com

Joann Fabric and Craft Stores
www.joann.com

Knitting-Warehouse.com
www.knitting-warehouse.com

M.C.G. Textiles
www.mcgtextiles.com

Michaels Stores, Inc.
www.michaels.com

Mielke's Fiber Arts, LLC
www.mielkesfiberarts.com

The Lamp Shop
www.lampshop.com

Specialty Locker Hooking Materials

Judi & Co.
www.judiandco.com
Specialty ribbons and yarns

Lantern Moon
www.lanternmoon.com
Silk Gelato yarn

Lion Brand Yarn
www.lionbrand.com
Yarns for locking medium and locker hooking

Primitive Gatherings Quilt Shop
www.primitivegatherings.us
Wool strips

Princess Mirah Design/Bali Fabrics, Inc.
www.princessmirah.com
Batik fabric strips

The Wool Peddler
www.recycledsilk.com
Sari ribbon and hand-dyed silk yarns

Yarn Market
www.yarnmarket.com
Yarns, ribbon yarns and fibers

Embellishments

Artbeads.com
www.artbeads.com
Beads

Artgirlz
www.artgirlz.com
Charms and felted wool embellishments

Art Institute Glitter, Inc.
www.artglitter.com
Glitter and glitter adhesive

FusionBeads.com
www.fusionbeads.com
Beads, embellishments and charms

Jacquard Products
www.jacquardproducts.com
Paints and polymer clay

Natural Touch Beads & Collectibles
www.naturaltouchbeads.com
Resin beads

Prima Marketing Inc.
www.primamarketinginc.com
Felt, silk and cotton floral embellishments

The Beadin' Path
www.beadinpath.com
Glass beads

Inspiration

Craft:
www.craftzine.com

Etsy
www.etsy.com

contributing artists

Cathren Britt

Cathren Britt is a studio/store owner and creative designer. Her Dancing Colours Studio is a warm and inviting space located in Carbondale, Colorado, where students are encouraged to have fun and take chances with their projects. Cathren believes that there is no greater treasure than a beautifully handmade gift. Visit her Web site at www.dancingcoloursstudio.com.

Kathleen Carpenter

Kathleen Carpenter is an expert needle crafter and has been locker hooking for 13 years. She pioneered the use of fabric strips with locker hooking and has published several instruction books with MCG Textiles. She teaches workshops in locker hooking, knitting, crochet and beadwork through her business, Spirited Hands. Kathleen lives in Edgewood, Washington, with her husband, two daughters and more pets than people.

Sherri Haab

Sherri Haab is a best-selling craft author with over twenty published books for adults and children to her credit. Sherri is a certified metal clay instructor, and leads numerous PMC and jewelry-making workshops nationwide. She is known for tracking trends in the craft industry and then educating consumers about how to use new products and techniques. Sherri studied illustration and loves to paint in her spare time. She resides in Springville, Utah, with her husband and three children. Visit Sherri's Web site at www.sherrihaab.com.

Cindy Sadowski

Cindy Sadowski is a lifelong artist and crafter and a student at Cathren Britt's Dancing Colours Studio. Cindy also runs a successful real estate firm in Carbondale, Colorado. Always excited about new materials and techniques, Cindy takes what she has learned from a workshop and adds her own creative touch!

index

add more fiber to your life

Pretty Little Felts

Mixed-Media Crafts to Tickle Your Fancy

Julie Collings

Create 24 projects using easy-to-follow instructions, and simple sewing and mixed-media techniques. Crafters of all skill levels will enjoy making pretty and functional items, such as a needle book, zippered pouch and flowers with crochet-edged petals.

ISBN 13: 978-1-60061-090-5
ISBN: 1-60061-090-0
paperback; 8" × 10"; 128 pages
Z1979

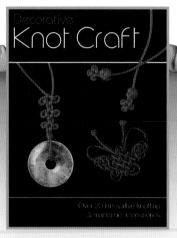

Decorative Knot Craft

Over 20 Innovative Knotting and Macramé Accessories

Kim Sang Lan

Includes over 20 jewelry and accessory projects and 11 techniques for a variety of knotting styles.

ISBN 13: 978-0-7153-2922-1
ISBN: 0-7153-2922-7
paperback; 8¼" × 10⅞"; 128 pages
Z2307

Craft Candy

Easy Projects to Stitch, Glue and Paint

Candace Marquette

Have fun learning the basics of sewing, hand stitching, leather weaving, painting and embellishing with this book full of fashion accessories and home décor. The 30+ projects incorporate low-sew methods and many types of embellishing materials.

ISBN 13: 978-0-89689-644-4
ISBN: 0-8969-644-7
paperback; 8¼" × 10⅞"; 128 pages
Z1948

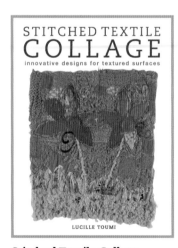

Stitched Textile Collage

Lucille Toumi

Stitched Textile Collage presents 25 appliquéd projects and offers a look at the use of textiles as a medium for creating innovative graphic artwork.

ISBN 13: 978-1-58180-988-6
ISBN: 1-58180-988-3
paperback; 8¼" × 10⅞"; 128 pages
Z0893

Canvas Remix

Alisa Burke

Mixed-media painting marries graffiti to produce 25 fun and funky projects that take canvas way beyond the stretcher bar to create unique jewelry, home accessories, tote bags and more.

ISBN 13: 978-1-60061-075-2
ISBN: 1-60061-075-7
paperback; 8¼" × 10⅞"; 128 pages
Z1844